HOW TO UNLEASH YOUR GREATNESS

Step into the Joy of living out your life assignment

ISBN: 9798838960528

SPECIAL FREE BONUS GIFT FOR YOU!

To help you to achieve more success, access the 'Bring Your Ideas to Life' course.

This course is 100% free and includes:

1. Importance of attention and focus and share how your brain often works against you when you're trying to do focused work.

2. Ways to design your work environment to eliminate distractions so you can focus on generating and developing ideas.

3. The role of systems and personal work habits in helping you to become a highly productive creative worker.

4. The crucial process of project management and how to lead a team in executing your idea into fully formed products or services.

How to Unleash Your Greatness

Look Higher Platform®

WHAT OTHERS ARE SAYING ABOUT
ROSE CHIKODZORE & HER STRATEGIES

I have known Rose for many years, and she is passionate and enthusiastic about empowering nurses in business. She is an excellent coach and public speaker. Her personal experience speaks volumes, and she recently shared her experience at an International Women's Day and it spoke to so many people. Rose is authentic and speaks with authority and to those who are thinking of starting their own business this book is full of strategies to empower them to transition into business by channelling their passions and transferable skills.

--Annie Barr MBE, MA, BSc Hons RGN PgCert (Coaching) INP ANP, Clinical Director, 'AB Health Group'

Rose Chikodzore is a gifted speaker & talented writer. She has a powerful story to tell and one that is well worth listening to - I highly recommend her to you and know she'll be a blessing to those whose life she touches.

--Angela Roth, CEO, 'Succeed from The Start.'

Rose is a coach and public speaker who is passionate about her service to healthcare professionals who are stressed and frustrated in their jobs. Her strategies empower them to transition into business by channelling their passions and transferable skills.
It was my pleasure to invite Rose to speak at the International Women's Day and Find Your Why 6th Anniversary Dinner in March 2022.

She captivated the audience with her authentic and honest words by sharing her own story, to help inspire the audience. I am sure that her book will do the same.

--Cheryl Chapman
Professional Why Finder & International Speaker, Mentor.

Rose is a coach and speaker who is passionate about her service to healthcare professionals who are stressed and frustrated in their jobs. Her passion to see her clients gain time and financial freedom stems from her nursing, midwife and leadership experience as well as seeing nurses' frustration first hand in several hospital settings. Rose's strategies empower them to transition into business by channelling their passions and transferable skills. Her strategies are well thought out and easy to follow to get you from where you are to where you need to go.

--Linda K. Zelnik
Leadership Coach, Speaker and Author of Burnout to Boom!

Rose Chikodzore is a woman of great insight, integrity and wisdom. She has an innate intuitive sense, leading people she coaches to break free of limitations and be transformed to unleash their greatest potential. Her coaching challenged me to set reasonable goals that created a brand-new chapter in my life. Absolutely amazing!

-- Mindy Geary
Retirement Coach, Author of 'Beyond the Money: Creating a Strong Retirement Plan: For All the Single Ladies'

MOTIVATE AND
INSPIRE OTHERS!

"Share This Book"

Special Order Discounts:

5-20 Books	£10.99/ Unit
21-99 Books	£9.99/ Unit
100-499 Books	£8.99/ Unit
500-999 Books	£7.99/ Unit
1.000+ Books	£6.99/ Unit

THE IDEAL PROFESSIONAL SPEAKER FOR YOUR NEXT EVENT!

Any organization that wants to develop their people to "THRIVE," needs to hire Rose Chikodzore for a keynote and/or workshop training!

If you're ready to overcome challenges, have major breakthroughs and achieve higher levels, then you will love having **Rose Chikodzore** as your speaker!

**To Enquire/ Book Rose for Your Next Event:
Email: rose@lookhigherplatform.co.uk**

THE IDEAL COACH FOR YOU!

**TO CONTACT OR BOOK ROSE CHIKODZORE
AS A COACH EMAIL:**

rose@lookhigherplatform.co.uk

DEDICATION

I would like to say a big thank you to my family for all the support, encouragement, and prayers. Your questions and enquiries kept me accountable and helped me to keep going.

To my brother Cosmas and sister Alice, thank you for leading the way in authorship.

My son Kudzalshe, daughter Evelyn and grandson Theophilus, thank you for allowing me the space to write and believing in me.

Shirley McKendry, my friend, thank you for carving out time out of your busy schedule to help with initial editing.

Lauren Roskilly for proof reading, graphics, and layout among other things.

Rose

ABOUT ROSE

Rose Chikodzore is a coach, trainer, public speaker. She inspires healthcare professionals who feel stressed and overwhelmed in their jobs, create thriving businesses by channelling what they love and know. Her passion is to bring transformation to her clients, so they gain, time, financial and location freedom.

Rose uses her story to move audiences when she speaks from the stage. Her message comes forth with authority. She created a step-by-step guide called The Profitable Passion Formula to demonstrate the path from employment to entrepreneurship. Which can be found here:

https://lookhigherplatform.coachesconsole.com

One of the places that Rose spoke at was in Manchester United Kingdom, for the 'Find Your Why' International Women's Day Event.

ACKNOWLEDGMENTS

Through the years, many have shared ideas, mentoring and support that has impacted my life, each in a different way. It's impossible to thank everyone and I apologize for anyone not listed. Please know, that I appreciate you greatly.

First and foremost, I want to thank God for the grace and ability to write this book. I am grateful to my son, Kudzaishe Chikodzore, my daughter Evelyn Sithole, grandson Theophilus Joshua, for encouraging and supporting me.
Nick and Megan Unsworth, James Malinchak, Louisa Shimamoto, Lauren Roskilly, Angela Lewis, Linda Zelnick, Cheryl Chapman, Angela Roth, Martha Robson, Lance Wallnau, John Milligan, John C Maxwell, Paul Martinelli, Andy Harrington, Ruth Driscoll, Melinda Cohen, Rob Moore.

A MESSAGE FOR YOU

This book will inspire you to step out and live out your life assignment. It highlights how true fulfilment comes from knowing that you did not shrink back but chose courage over fear to serve others. Many people spend their lifetimes in jobs they hate and work with people they don't like due to fear of leaving their comfort zone.

The examples in this book are from a wide spectrum of young and old, from different countries. The one common trait they had was they were bold to follow through their beliefs and convictions to step into entrepreneurship, overcome the challenges and achieve their dreams. One example is a social enterprise, but the characteristics are similar.

Excuses and ruling yourself out are twin challenges which are prevalent to stop you in your tracks. Reading how others overcame have been discussed here and the ways to proceed despite them.

There's a plethora of people and tools at your disposable to go for your goals. The sky is the limit. Go for gold!

"Whether you think you can or think you can't, you're right"
Henry Ford

HOW TO UNLEASH YOUR GREATNESS

Step into the Joy of living out your life assignment

Table of Contents

CHAPTER 1

THERE'S GREATNESS IN YOU

It's the 20th of September 1986. I'm in a large white walled room with air conditioning. On my left is my colleague Jane who is watching every move I make. On my right and a bit behind me is Sarah, holding a sterile green cotton cloth in her hands. I can smell antiseptic, but there is another smell which is typical of this room where we all are.

In front of me is Judy. Sweat is pouring down her face and she is dozing slightly but suddenly wakes up and lets out a loud cry. She pushes with all her might and, suddenly someone else enters the room. They are very rude; they don't wait for others to finish talking but assault our ears with incessant crying. We are all overjoyed. I quickly cut the cord and hand the baby boy to Sarah who lays the baby on Judy's chest. Judy is crying and laughing at the same time.

She looks very tired but relieved. The labour took ten hours, and she was on the brink of having a caesarean section. The doctors were worried that the baby might be too big and both Judy and the baby were getting tired.

Her husband could not make the birth as he is serving in the army, but he managed to get time off at the last minute and will arrive tonight. We are all excited for this family because of their new bundle of joy.

We are all one big family in the maternity unit, and we support each other as the birth of a baby can be a matter of life and death. But everyone can relax now. For a moment I'm reminded of my first few weeks working on the labour ward. I would be so tense during the birth of a baby. As at the time, I had not learnt to untangle my emotions and empathy as a new midwife. Goodness knows who pushed more, the mother or me!

My mind jolts back to the present, to this room. We start to think of that cup of tea we are all desiring once mother and baby are settled. We laugh and joke but all the time watching that mother and baby are ok. Soon, they are settled, all cleaned up and the new arrival is nestling in Judy's arms while she drinks a cup of tea.

This is our usual day, seeing babies come into the world. Every delivery is different and has its own drama, but we all enjoy working here. Most days things are ok, and we have a healthy mother and baby, but occasionally there's a dash to the operating theatre when labour becomes complicated, and the medics and nurses are in a hurry to act swiftly and save both.

Have you had any highlights in your life? Those instances that stay with you for years?

For me it was working in maternity. From about age 5, I dreamt of being a nurse and looking after sick people. This desire would not go away even though I was always freaked out from visiting our local clinic. I always equated it with pain – from injections. During my childhood, antibiotics were almost always in injection form. As if that was not enough, I also needed to have various vaccinations.

But in my heart of hearts, I knew that nursing was the job I wanted to do when I was old enough. I suppose it was probably because adults were not on the receiving end of it, because all my mum had to do was to place my legs between hers to keep me still while the nurse gave me an injection. My siblings faced the same fate. She was the only one who left the clinic unscathed and dry eyed!

After a series of events, I ended up at a nursing training school when I turned 18. I thoroughly enjoyed my training even though this was during the time when some ward sisters were ogres! They made you feel daunted in their presence and that you should rethink whether you wanted to continue with your quest to be a nurse. Fortunately, they were in the minority and that allowed you to enjoy work on most of the wards and endure the few.

The other hard area was coming face to face with the suffering of humanity as a teenager. Some of the conditions made your heart break but you learnt to toughen up. I suppose it's a bit like young people joining the army, only less challenging. I remember one of my colleagues who passed out when she watched the Ward Sister pass a nasogastric tube on a patient who was being prepared for theatre. In time she learnt to do this procedure too with no problems. It was all one big learning curve.

So, I worked as a midwife for 25 years. Most of that time was spent on the labour ward. The greatest joy was seeing a little person emerge into the world. When everything was ok, there was a loud cry to announce their arrival. At other times, some intervention was needed before that cry was heard. It's the only ward in the hospital where you admit one person and discharge two or more if there is multiple pregnancy. That's the miracle of life!

Later in my career, I worked on the other end of the spectrum of life, in adult and elderly care. I had moved to the United Kingdom, and this opportunity was readily available. I was hesitant to take it because I didn't think I would enjoy this change. But soon enough I took to it like a duck to water! I enjoyed looking after the elderly, especially when they were cheeky and had some quacks! We often had uproarious times and enjoyed listening to their stories about growing up during the war, school system and careers.

By the way, there is a cry on either side of life, one is announcing arrival, the other is a cry of triumphal exit, of a life well lived and a legacy to leave behind after disembarking from this life. Unfortunately, the exit is not always accompanied by a cry of triumph, but sometimes the regret of what could have been. The list ranges from relationships, family, marriage, career, charity, and fun.

Rocking chair story....

Have you ever thought about what stories you will tell your grandchildren?

Imagine yourself sitting on the patio or veranda, rocking back and forth in your chair. You can hear someone mowing the lawn next door, smell the newly mown grass and you start to reminisce. Will the stories you tell be ones of courage and adventure? Or will they be about how you missed great opportunities in life? I sincerely hope it will be about the former.

A group coach once asked us what our rocking chair story would be. It was a sobering thought. Most people regret, not areas where they attempted to do things and failed, but those where they developed cold feet and failed to go into doors that opened before them and seize the opportunities. Do you know that most of these opportunities never come back? An opportunity, like an idea, is short lived. Successful people know this and are quick to make decisions. Nick Unsworth's favourite saying is, "make the decision, then make it right."

You don't want to reach the twilight years, with regret, but with stories of a life well lived! Not only that but with testimonies of people whose lives you touched and made better. At this stage in your life being risk-averse looks different from when you were young. You can clearly see that you missed the boat but cannot change things now due to advanced age, failing health and strength. That thought has a bitter taste to it!

But things don't have to be that way for you. You still have some years ahead of us and can make use of these with intentionality and deliberateness. It is still possible to change your mind about being risk averse and go after your dreams. The time to put your feet to your ideas and get that business started is now. There is so much fulfilment in serving and adding value to others.

On this page write down ten ideas you have had over the years.

Choose the top three.

Of the three, choose the one that most resonates with you and start with that one.

_____

_____

_____

_____

_____

_____

_____

_____

_____

_____

_____

_____

_____

_____

_____

CHAPTER 2

GREATNESS ON THE INSIDE

It is my firm belief that there is greatness on the inside of every person that is born into this world. Our fingerprints are different, DNA too, because we are unique individuals and are not clones.

Everyone is born with an assignment and finding that and living it out is our greatest achievement. This will bring, not only fulfilment, but also a great example for others to follow. You were born to roar, don't settle for a meow! Instead, be like that cat who looked at himself in the mirror and saw a lion, because that is who you are.

It's time to unleash your potential because there's greatness in you! There's gold on the inside of you – waiting to be mined, polished, and served to others. You are not just a number or a statistic no matter the circumstances of your birth, family background or country you came from. It doesn't matter whether you were born and raised on a council estate, or in a palace. Everyone carries a potential that is waiting to be unleashed!

You might ask; "But how do I find out what greatness is on the inside of me?"

Here's a simple way to find out what your gifts/ talents are: -

Questions to ask yourself:

What makes me sing? What lights up my life?

What don't I get tired of doing?

What problems am I always solving for my family and friends?

What problems do I find easy to solve?

What problems do I enjoy solving?

Let me tell you about my 8-year-old grandson, Theo. He's a numbers guy!

Why do I say so?

He will tell you exactly what time he woke up, he's like, "I got up at 7:55 today, yesterday I was a bit late, I got up at 8:15." When he was younger, he visited me with my son. I have two couches and there were 4 cushions on the one couch and two on the one he and I were sitting on. He surveyed the situation and took the two of the cushions from his dad, he gave me one and took the other. These are just tiny clues that add up to see what one's natural learning is.

Once, we were at a holiday resort and went down a lot of steps to the beach and he remarked, "I'm tired we have just gone down 27 steps!" Another day we had a quiz at church, we were divided into 2 groups so we could name the countries whose flags were being shown. After the quiz he whispered to me that there were 43 countries in the quiz. Our team was concentrating on wanting to beat the other team by naming more countries than them, but he wanted to know the number of countries in the quiz! His dad is a numbers guy too and studied Actuary and Mathematics at university, so I think there's some inherited trait there!

What about you? What trends do you see in yourself or your family?

For some it might not be a fun thing but alleviation of suffering like working with orphans, the homeless, abandoned animals, or poor communities. That passion is what will drive you. No matter what obstacles you face, the fire on the inside will carry you through any challenge and hardship!

There is fulfilment in being true to yourself and your life calling. A sense of being on the right path. The transformation that occurs in others lights up your life and brings meaning to life.

Have you ever noticed that just having money alone does not fully satisfy you? How many celebrities, that you know of, have had issues with drink, drugs, depression or can't seem to settle in one marriage? I'm not advocating that being poor makes you happy. No, it doesn't. Given a choice you would rather be wealthy and sad than poor and sad. Why, because money gives you options, even for treatment. No one was ever meant to be persistently in survival mode.

Pursuing your passion and using the right business model can result in generational wealth creation. This is not a given, there are no guarantees, but a good work ethic, mentoring and community go a long way to ensure this. As you serve others, you experience fulfilment and a sense of purpose.

> *"The two most important days in your life are, the day you are born and the day you find out why."*
> *Mark Twain*

What if you are still unsure?

Did you know that sometimes, the most important thing you need to do is to STOP?

I remember the story of a coach from America. He had a very large business and was always busy getting new clients and forging ahead with the vision for his company. But then he suddenly became ill, with high blood pressure. The illness was so bad that he was experiencing severe nose bleeds with clots!

So, his physician admitted him to hospital and advised bed rest in conjunction with all the treatment he was getting. It took a whole month for him to get back to his usual blood pressure even though the nosebleeds stopped much earlier. He stated when he was on bedrest, he initially fretted about his business but later decided to plan and delegate tasks to his team. That month his business did better than when he was working in the business. Now he was a visionary with clarity because by stopping he was able to plan and strategize.

I don't think he never used to plan before, but being away from the day-to-day hustle allowed him to plan with intentionality. This reminds me of an African proverb that says, "If you want to go fast, go alone, if you want to go far go with others." By involving his team and delegating, his business expanded.

You may have probably heard advice: on working *on* your business, rather than *in* your business. The former keeps you busy getting daily tasks done, while the later allows you to have a projection of vision to know where you want to direct your business. It's a given that at the beginning you tend to be 'jack of all trades' in your business. But, with time you can start to bring others in and form your team.

We live in a world that is at a fast pace. We are an impatient generation who want instant results. Think of fast broadband, quick dialling, 2-minute noodles, microwave meals, chopped onions from the supermarket, instant mash, the list goes on and on!

However, the above story shows us that planning and reflecting is essential for better productivity. It allows you to work smarter, not harder! If you are like me, you could say "but that man already had a business, I don't!" Yes, this might be so, but the same principle applies even at the beginning. Normally we do not give ourselves credit for our skills and abilities. But sitting down to reflect and giving yourself permission to dream is helpful in accessing the real desires of your life.

Permission to dream; grab hold of it!

CHAPTER 3

WHAT ARE THE HINDRANCES?

Some people go on to mine gold, but others will forever be planning to do something about it. The richest man in biblical times well said, 'The slothful says there is a lion out there'.

For most people it's not so much the sloth but lack of awareness. You don't know what you don't know, right?

For me, the light bulb moment came when I was in a business seminar held by the late Dr Myles Munroe. His question was, 'What is the wealthiest place on earth?' We gave answers like, 'Silicone Valley, diamond mines and others. But to everyone's surprise he said the richest place on earth is the cemetery. We were all wide eyed! Really?!

Here's part of an excerpt about how he taught on the importance of living out your life assignment:

> If you are 40, 50, 60 years old and do not know why you are living, and still do not know your purpose, or why you came to this planet, know this: You were not born just to make a living. You are here to live out an assignment on this planet. You were born to make a difference and to make the world a better place.
>
> Many people die without manifesting this seed of greatness, however. They will take that gift to the grave without using it. They will be buried

with untapped treasure. The wealthiest place on earth is not the gold mines of South America or the diamond mines of South Africa. It is not the oil fields of Iran, Iraq, Kuwait, or the silver mines of Central America. The wealthiest place on earth is the cemetery. It holds the treasures that people never served to humanity.

It is wealthy because buried in the cemetery are books that were never written. In the graveyard is music that no one had a chance to hear, songs that were never sung! The graveyard is filled with magazines that were never published. The cemetery is filled with businesses that were never opened. What a tragedy!" -God Seeker TV

Wow! It's very sobering. Normally you don't get people who speak to you in a deep place. This is very evident in the world we now live in with all the busyness and needing to get things done. Add social media to this and you have a superficial way of relating where you can just use an emoji or a GIF in response to a friend's post! But to really get to grips with your value and what you bring to others' needs, some thinking space is required. In addition to this, being motivated and encouraged by those who have walked the path you are embarking on, can be very helpful.

Next are some ways that you may be minimising your worth. If you pay attention to conversations, someone may commend what another is wearing. Sometimes acknowledgement is the response, however most of the time the response is like, 'Oh I bought this in the sale, or it's a hand-me -down from my sister'

I used to respond in similar ways until a friend pointed it out. This made me realise there were many instances where I had tried to go back in the shadows, as it were, instead of thanking whoever was commending my attire or another skill. Have you ever had instances like that? If not, you are in the minority. Keep it up!

I read an article by a blogger in Northern Ireland who stated that in the UK we are less likely to accept commendations than in the US. He said when he was growing up, he and his friends regarded the rich as proud and mean. As a result, anyone who found themselves being successful was at risk of alienation. This reminded me of the analogy of crabs in a bucket. If one starts crawling up to the rim, it never makes it because the rest will pull it back!

Now this being pulled back is not necessarily from the outside in most cases but from between your ears. Thoughts like;

"Who am I to think I can be a successful businessperson?"

"None of my family have ever done this",

"I come from a council estate."

"We are all employees and that's it!"

This shows that you need to have different beliefs and thoughts from the regular guy! Your beliefs drive your thoughts and, in turn, your way of life. What if things could be different. Who says they can't be? What choice would you rather make, to go with the naysayers or with your deepest passion? Who put that passion inside you? Why is it not in your brother or friend? Do you have a responsibility to live it out? Or are you going to snuff out the flame and just do business as usual?

How do you change beliefs and thoughts? This can be achieved through reading books written by people who have had success in the area you want to go. Mentoring and coaching, being among other entrepreneurs, hearing their stories of trying, failing then finally succeeding will go a long way to encourage you in your journey. Just learning and not acting is very limited. Nothing substitutes experience in achieving results.

There is an old proverb told by John C. Maxwell in his book, *The 15 Invaluable Laws of Growth* –

When I was a kid, one of my father's favourite riddles to us went like this: Five frogs are sitting on a log. Four decide to jump off. How many are left?

The first time he asked me, I answered, "One."

"No," he responded, "Five. Why? Because there is a difference between deciding and doing."

Write down what you want your life to look like in two years from now. Just write without stopping to think.

CHAPTER 4

FEAR OF THE UNKNOWN

'Fear of the unknown is the greatest fear of all'
- Yvon Chouinard

Fear by its very nature can be very crippling. It forms an invisible wire in your path that dares you to cross. This wire is very real to you, and everyone experiences it in a different way. In its worst manifestation there can be panic attacks which can mimic a heart attack, throwing up and even fainting. Unfortunately, some people have been so crippled by such severe anxiety that they cannot even leave the house!

I just want to make a differentiation here. There is the anxiety that is due to mental health conditions, which is horrible. But, fortunately, in medicine, there are ways to tackle this. For example, Cognitive Behavioural Therapy (CBT) and other interventions.

I'm addressing the fear of stepping out to do something new. Fear of the unknown is so irrational in that you might even end up enjoying the task or experience!

The only person who doesn't fail is the one who never tried. Many people who have faced their fears have been pleasantly surprised to find out that their life assignment folded out as soon as they crossed the terror barrier.

Suzanne, a business mentor once told us how she threw up on the first day she organised a live event. She went on to do the training and has been influential in many businesses since. She would never have marketed her services if she had chickened out. Instead, she would have short-changed not just herself, but also the target audience that she influences and empowers.

When I first heard Dr Myles Munroe, I made up my mind to pursue my passion with all that I possess. Has it been easy? Have I been consistent? The answer to both is, no, of course not! The path has been winding, uneven and rough. Things have been harder and taken longer than I thought. Many times, I dropped the ball and got distracted but that quote "Richest place on earth" had put a fire on the inside of me, despite times where the fire was just smouldering, it never got extinguished!

My mindset has worked against me more often than I dare to admit. I have lacked personal accountability, have let myself off the hook too many times and chosen the path of least resistance. Many times, I was tempted to give up but as I looked around, even online, there were a lot of people who refused to give up on their dreams. So that has spurred me on and kept me going.

Have you ever been in a place where you knew that you had to just keep going? You felt that your knees were grazed, and you were limping but the spark on the inside kept you pushing forward? What was the feeling when you got to the finishing line?

> *'Fear kills more dreams than failure ever will.' – Suzy Kassem*

'Far better is it to dare mighty things, to win glorious triumphs, even though checked by failure, than to rank with those poor spirits who neither enjoy nor suffer much, because they live in a grey twilight that knows not victory nor defeat.' - Theodore Roosevelt

A bible teacher, Joyce Meyer teaches on 'Doing it Afraid' which I find very encouraging because fear must let you go as you step out and up. Successful speakers report feeling fear too, but the difference with them is they don't let the fear stop them! They have learnt the skills to leverage the fear to their advantage and continue to impact audiences. Competitive athletes report experiencing fear too, but they use it to their advantage.

In 1991, I was asked to report on findings of a research project I had done with others at the university of Zimbabwe. There were scholars and research professors from Zimbabwe and Sweden. I was so nervous and was not able to enjoy my lunch, because I was speaking after. There was a churning in my stomach, and I had to visit the toilet twice! Really, Rose? Yes, but when I spoke, I felt I had done well despite the horrible symptoms of fear that I had felt.

Fast forward to 2022, I was speaking at an International Women's event in Manchester, England. I asked the convener to slot me in before lunch. She understood, because she had told us how she never used to eat in her early days as an international speaker. Surprisingly, I was calm this time around because now I knew it was fear that had plagued me in 1991. I felt in control and was able to share my story and service with authority.

Going forward, I know that fear is a feeling that your brain brings up to warn you in the same way it would if you were getting to the edge of a high cliff and there was danger due to the sheer drop. Every time you step out to do something new, your brain goes, 'Wait, you've not been this way before. Are you sure you want to go on?' The brain is just doing its job by trying to get your attention but should never be allowed to stop your ventures. It's an inbuilt survival mode kicking in.

So, now it's time to step out anyhow! The world is waiting to experience your product/service. Will you keep them waiting? If not you, then who? If not now, then when?

I am inviting you to a journey of self-discovery, full of surprises. No one should ever feel they have arrived in life, thus my invitation is to live out your life assignment.

Let us journey together.

Write down any instances you have felt fear. What were the symptoms? How did you deal with them?

CHAPTER 5

FEAR OF FAILURE

"Everything you want is on the other side of fear." -Jack Canfield.

This is one of the worst kinds of fears. It reminds me of my grandson on his 7th birthday. He had a Nintendo switch as a birthday present. So, we were in two bowling teams. I was the eldest and least one expected to win, but I did. My grandson on the other hand, despite being extremely competitive and skilled in most games, just couldn't get the hang of how to swing the ball. He gave up and was quite crestfallen.

It took his aunty to hold his hand and help him bowl for him to get back in the game. Thankfully, this ended well because he managed to grab some of the skill and was able to stay in the game till the end. Normally, he is great at building Lego, understanding technology and the like but someone took pictures of him when he was sad and refusing to play. Every time I look at the pictures now, I see how it's so unlike his character to be so vexed.

This happens to us too, as adults. As mentioned in the previous chapter, anything that looks like it's too hard, our brain tells us to sidestep or to keep out. The difference between successful people and unsuccessful is that successful people will do things despite fear. They leverage their fear to achieve greatness, as seen in the previous chapter.

31

So, you need to agree that this thing is unfamiliar but let's push the boundaries here, because to obtain what you have not obtained before, you need to do something you have never done before. The other thing is that behavioural scientists report that the brain is hardwired to protect us. It is not wired for adventure, but to keep us safe. And that's why you find that many people struggle when it comes to doing something for the very first time, going into territory we've never gone into before.

One of these areas is public speaking. You probably know that some people prefer to die than to speak in public! Others go as far as to say if they were asked to give a eulogy at the funeral of a friend, they would rather be the one in the box than to stand up to speak! How amazing is that?

So, when you know this, it becomes easier to do what's needed despite feeling fear. The feelings that you're sensing is your brain trying to protect you but you yourself know that you need to be doing new things, new skills, and new adventures.

In entrepreneurship there's a need to learn new skills like effective communication in marketing. I have heard some of my clients say, "I don't want to put myself out there." When you think of it, it's like they are talking about some nether land that is dark and has wild animals lurking there. Yet it's something like doing a live video on Facebook or any social media channel. How do I know the feelings of anxiety about this? Because I used to feel the same but with continual practice the fear soon gives way and you become like a duck taking to water. Fair enough, there are other people who will never feel comfortable being on camera, no matter what. Thankfully there are other ways to do the videos without showing your face.

One other way to get past fear is to know that your message is not about you. It's all about your audience. Knowing this helps you to get past your fears to make sure that your message is heard by the people who are languishing in a problem that you have the answer to. For me that was a game changer! I had to tell myself to get out of the way of my own destiny. If you have not yet done this, now is a good time!

Have you ever watched how the army trains the SAS? With each passing day the mentors watch you closely for any sign of fear. Once that becomes evident, they expel you otherwise you will be a liability to your colleagues on dangerous assignments.

During the recent war in the Ukraine, we saw the fearlessness of the ordinary men and women defending their country. Everyday people signed up and held guns for the very first time in their life.

I will never forget a woman whose hands were being held by the trainer while showing her how to aim at the target. Boldness and courage win the day before skill does. One farmer used a tractor to tow away an army vehicle! The stories are numerous!

Here are some nuggets from successful businesspeople:

Jim Rohn famously said, "Don't wish it was easier! Wish you were better. Don't wish for less problems wish for more skills." Phew! That's hard and it's uphill. Is it exhilarating when you finally crack the code and find your way to what was a dream only at first? You better believe it!

Thomas Eddison, creating the light bulb, failing 10, 000 times before finally having that light. When the reporter taunted how he had failed 10, 000 times, his reply was classic, "I have not failed. I've just found 10,000 ways that won't work." How life became easier and different with lights!

John C. Maxwell, "No one ever got to the top by mistake. You need uphill thinking. It's easy to slide downhill, but uphill living requires uphill thinking."

The other gremlin that rears as a twin of fear of failure is fear of rejection. As a businessperson you cannot get emotionally entangled with the result of your sale. Can you imagine a stewardess on a flight serving a meal? She offers you tea and you decline. It would be very weird for that stewardess to be downcast because you didn't accept tea from her.

After all she brought the best tea bags the airline has ever purchased and you also had premium milk to go with it, but that passenger said, "No!" And she runs to the back so that you cannot see her tears. When she comes back, other passengers ask her if she is ok and she points to you. That's getting fixated, isn't it? Yet some entrepreneurs worry about rejection so much they stop in their tracks rather than move forward to let their target audience know about their awesome product or service.

It's time to kick these twin gremlins into the trash can where they belong and serve your community. The transformation, testimonials and client stories will energise you like never before.

Go for gold!

CHAPTER 6

FEAR OF SUCCESS

This fear is usually associated with other issues like fear of losing friends, loneliness, inability to keep up with the success. Think of lottery winners who had success for a few years and then lost all their money after a few years.

"Fear of success?" You might wonder. What does that look like? Doesn't every person desire success in whatever they set out to do? Recently I read a story in a business periodical about a retired gentleman who started a social enterprise which was in line with his passion. In time the enterprise began to thrive, and investors came on board. Soon there were dinners and presentations as people were excited at how this man was bringing transformation in the community.

Due to the anxiety that he began experiencing because of the success of the business, the man had to retire and seek counselling. He was happy enough to run an enterprise that was small and felt fulfilment in what he did. But when growth and visibility came, he found that he could not handle it. His counsellor, on digging deep, found out that he had been raised by a father who scorned success. His father had not graduated from High School and whenever this gentleman came home with good grades his father was verbally abusive. His father hurt him because of his own insecurities and failure to achieve. So, the retiree said he had always sought jobs that had little visibility throughout his working life to avoid any wounding of his soul.

You look at this and you think, 'Wow, I never thought success could negatively affect anyone. But the counsellor said the problem was very real and he had to work with the retiree to deal with the root of his problem.

Fear of success might manifest itself as a tendency to aim low. What do I mean by that? If you are afraid of success or of putting yourself out there, as people say, then aiming low is a form of self-preservation so that there won't be any chance of failure. In other words, you could make the goal so low, so that there's no chance of failure. You know you can hit it, no matter what happens, and it is bound to be successful. That inherent fear of success is fear of doing new things or being in new territory, so you prefer to be in your comfort zone. You don't want to step out of your comfort zone even though it looks like this thing is going to be more successful.

This might seem strange, but there are people who like the known and familiar compared to going on an adventure and discovering new horizons. A pastor from Glasgow, once said, "My ambition was, when I grow up, I want to have a 3 bedroomed semi-detached house, marry a wife and have 2 children, full stop." He didn't think of anything else besides that. Fortunately, as time went on his mindset shifted, he pushed the envelope and ended up doing some amazing things in his life. He pastored a church and trained up leaders who went on to replicate the work in other towns and nations.

One of our colleagues who attends the same coaching program as me, told us how her daughter is ashamed of the life they live. The colleague is African American, a doctor, and her daughter wants to be like her friends! She is well provided for but feels guilty about it and wants to fit in with her peers.

Perhaps because of teenage peer pressure she feels that way. But I was at a business retreat once where a very successful woman who is a millionaire did not want this to be known. She employs over 200 people but was struggling with sharing her achievements even to a group of 6!

Like I have said, the light bulb for me came on in a business meeting. Looking back prior to this I could see the rudimentary flashes of what I was supposed to take up. However, it took someone who was a seasoned mentor and thought leader to pull that out of me, as it were.

Would you say you have had problems with fear of success? Or would you say for you it's fear of failure? Or a fear of the unknown?

As human beings we were born to be successful. We are wired to excel and impact other people. There's so much on the inside of you that you're still to discover. And that goes for many of us. I don't know if there are any successful businesspeople or billionaires who can tell you, 'I've arrived, I'm totally happy there's nothing else that I want to do or that I am aiming for,' because that's not in our DNA.

We were made for greatness. We were made for more. Once you reach one peak there's another one to aim for. This reminds me of when we climbed a mountain called Schiehallion in Scotland. It is the second highest and has more than one peak. Before we reached the first peak, I was thinking we had nearly arrived and could not wait for a chance to rejoice, take a selfie, and then have a nice cup of tea.

But to my dismay when we reached this peak, I saw there was another peak, I thought 'Oh my gosh there are two peaks, when we get there, we can do what I thought we could do here. After we had just gone a short distance, we met people who were coming down and one guy said to us, 'I hope you know that this mountain has got false peaks, so you're not even there yet, you need to be strong.'

I had to give myself a pep talk to be able to keep going, because I wasn't expecting this. The worst thing was that the last hour and a half or so of climbing that mountain there were boulders only and nothing else. This was hard on weary feet. Long story short, we did manage to get to the top of this mountain. It was exhilarating, the view below was stunning. All in all, it took us 3 hours to go up and 3 to get down.

This is what happens in life, by the time you reach one peak, your mindset has shifted. You see more possibilities, bigger opportunities. You have met a lot of challenges along the way, and you've learnt how to problem solve. You've developed resilience and learnt how to keep going even when you don't feel like it. All that has worked in your favour by enlarging your mindset.

Therefore, you need not fear failure. Continue to aim high and remember to, 'Do it afraid!' Aim high, don't just settle for the low hanging fruit. Have you noticed how an elephant will stand on its back legs to reach for those top soft leaves? You are meant to eat from the top of the tree like a giraffe or an elephant! That's who you are. Are you ready for this?

Time to stretch, be bold and courageous!

CHAPTER 7

IMPOSTOR SYNDROME

"Impostor syndrome is a persistent doubt concerning one's abilities or accomplishments accompanied by fear of being exposed as a fraud despite evidence of one's ongoing success." - Merriam – Webster dictionary.

According to a publication by Psychreg (2021), in the UK 77% of people stated they have experienced impostor syndrome. Here are some of the symptoms that the article listed: -

- Doubting yourself.
- Being unable to accurately assess your competence and skills.
- Attributing your success to external factors.
- Being afraid of disappointment.

"I'm not good enough." "Who am I that people should listen to me/ buy from me?" Have you ever said these words to yourself? Where do they stem from, do you think? What great feats have you stopped yourself from doing by listening to that voice? What business ideas, joint venture offers have you let pass because of that feeling?

Quite a lot of people struggle with this psychological feeling in the workplace or in business and yet anyone can set up a business. The internet has changed the way buying and selling is done. There are no gatekeepers online and you can work from any country on earth providing you have reliable internet.

Each day millionaires are being created. Even teenagers are becoming millionaires with the most unlikely of businesses. By thinking outside the box and listening to the heart rather than your head, the sky's the limit to what you can achieve!

You can't turn the news on without hearing about the high cost of living and the recession, but during a recession the opportunities are endless. There will always be people in need of your service/product. The question is, do you believe this? Which side would you like to be; with the naysayers or the go- getters?

Starting out in business is not easy, but it is doable. Other people with less education and finances have done this so can you. The doubts will creep up on you, but there is hope and there is help!

Some of the ways that help overcome limiting beliefs include investing in personal development, mentorship, coaching and mindset training. Many successful people read a book a week and are in community, through masterminds. When you journey with like-minded people there's support, accountability, and encouragement.

Investing in the above will go a long way to prevent you from throwing in the towel. But even with support, encouragement and accountability, the most successful people have felt like giving up. The difference is that community can help you to get back on track. There's nothing like having partners who will call you up for what you promised to do. This is invaluable in business.

The other thing that you might overlook is that you have gained invaluable skills in education, work, and most of these are transferable. Generally, most people underestimate their value and what they can give to others. This is usually down to people not receiving affirmation regarding their gifts or talents when they were growing up.

Instead, words from people in influential positions like parents or teachers, cripple in later life. Have you ever heard someone say, "You'll never amount to anything", "Education is not the place for you" or "you're too dull!" As a result, one can end up believing the *lie* that they are not very gifted and have nothing to offer.

Have you ever heard someone being commended on a shirt, blouse they were wearing? Then the answer to that kind comment is, wait for it... "Oh it's a hand-me-down from my sister", "I bought it in the sale", "it's very old" or "I've had it for 5 years!"

I like what Dr Mike Murdock from the Wisdom Centre says, 'You are paid for the problems you solve.'

What problem were you born to help solve? What medical breakthrough will come through your study and research? Which curriculum for children will you come up with that will radicalise the education system?

The list is endless!

Michael Jordan did not qualify for the basketball team. Instead, he started off picking up balls. He was the first to get to the pitch and the last to leave, practised more than any other person. This is a man just like you and me but his passion for the game drove him beyond other people. He did what other people were not willing to do. No wonder he became a legend! Anyone could have done what he was doing, but they didn't. They didn't even need to be the one to initiate but they could just copy what he was doing and become who he became. The difference between him and these other people, is mindset. He was a go-getter, and nothing was going to stand in the way of his dreams. This is something you can do too!

Les Brown got his break by speaking on radio when the presenter did not turn up! He then went on to become one of the best speakers in the world! The way he tells this story is very hilarious. He was ready for the opportunity before it turned up. Well, his job was to make tea for the presenters and other bosses. In his heart, he knew that wasn't the end, he was aiming to be one of the presenters. This was even despite a bad experience in school where he was 'written off.' But, as soon as that opportunity came, he was quick to grab it and did not allow anything to stand in the way! Today Les Brown is known as one of the best speakers of all time.

What are you called to be and what are you willing to sacrifice? What hoops are you willing to go through and what challenges are you willing to face so that you can step into who you were made to be?

Uber changed the way taxis operate, by using GPS, no cash, and efficient fast service. One taxi driver said, "Uber managed to eliminate the problem with people who were legless after spending the whole night drinking, ordering a taxi and 'discovering 'they had no money on the other end.' It also eliminated people who don't possess a bank card, thus screening their clientele in a smart way."

This shows that you do not need to reinvent the wheel sometimes. But look for gaps in a service/product and then make it more user friendly.

Each of us is born different, our fingerprints are different. You have a sweet spot with honey that the world is waiting for you to serve. Another way to look at it is:

You have diamonds in the toughest state on the inside of you, but you need to:

- Recognise their presence
- Learn how to mine them
- Polish them
- Then turn them into beautiful ladies.

CHAPTER 8

DISTRACTIONS

In recent years many have found that distraction is a sly thief. How many times have you decided to just check social media quickly and then get on with the assignment or house chore? Before you know it, two hours have passed because you got drawn in with the stories, the likes, and comments!

Daily we have various responsibilities towards family, caring, preparing meals, shopping. The list is endless.

So, it becomes imperative to plan for success. Setting targets and rewarding yourself is a good way towards good productivity. Reading up on the habits of successful people is also key. Tony Robbins says, "success leaves clues." So, by watching how other entrepreneurs win in a world that is in a mad rush can be very helpful.

Here are some ways to overcome distractions:

- Morning routine
- Journaling
- Rhythms of Work and Rest
- Accountability
- Environment

Morning Routine

A few years ago, my then six-year-old grandson asked, 'Gramma, what's your morning routine?' I was surprised at how he knows a language that I didn't know even in my 30s! I thought he had probably overheard some adult discussing this. Fair enough, while I was a student, I knew that my best time for study was in the morning and that I needed a good night's sleep for this to work. Even when I started working, I kept to this sort of pattern. If I had a few late nights in a week, I needed to catch up by going to bed at 8pm one day a week for my brain to reroute and focus properly. But words like 'morning routine' were alien to me.

Each person's routine is different because we are all made uniquely. It is important to have a plan for the week or for the month. This frees up time for the rest of the day rather than trying to plan daily.

As a Christian the morning is a good time for me to prepare spiritually first through prayer, worship bible reading and journaling. I like my personal space to go through this. However, this can be done with others, as a couple or family.

For some people, other ways to start the day are exercise like swimming, walking the dog and listening to motivational material is good as well as it can help towards getting yourself ready to win. Having a routine is a great way to keep on track. If you do something for

90 days, it will likely develop into a habit and will be easier to adhere to.

Having a tidy office, especially if you work from home, is also very helpful. A tidy environment is conducive to productivity because precious time is not wasted by looking for items or important paperwork.

Keeping away from emails and phone calls and texts and social media is another great way to preserve your brain bandwidth for the things that matter the most. Some successful businesspeople have personal assistants that answer their emails and only refer to the emails that they really need to attend to.

Journaling and Reflection

There is a need for robust planning on the front end of the day and reflecting at the end; reviewing what worked and what didn't work. The use of journals – especially ones that are prepared for keeping on track. I have started using the 'Be Fulfilled Journal,' after Mike Kim mentioned it in one of his posts and have found it to be very useful! It even tracks how much water you have drunk, what relationships to nurture, exercise as well as work and focus. There is a planning section for the morning and a review section for the night.

Rhythms of Work and Rest

One other method that aids productivity, avoids procrastination is the Pomodoro Technique. Pomodoro is Italian for tomato. This technique was devised by Francesco Cirillo.

Ankit Patel says that "The Pomodoro Technique is a time management method that aims to maximise productivity through focused sessions of work. Tasks are divided in intervals of 25 minutes, also called a pomodoro session. After each interval, the worker takes a short break for about 5 minutes. During the session, the worker provides complete focus on the task and only on the task. It is effective in avoiding distractions and gaining maximum productivity due to its regular obligatory breaks. It is also popular because it is simple to learn and portable in different work scenarios. The Pomodoro method is the principle of many smartphone productivity apps today to help all types of workers, especially knowledge workers, maximise productivity."

Accountability

Chad Allen, a book author, and coach sets aside an hour some weeks for his clients to come together online and work on their manuscripts, marketing funnels or any other aspect of work that moves the business needle. I once joined this group when I was part of his membership and found it very helpful. At the end of the session each person shared what they were working on and how they felt about having acted. I believe that it's beneficial to have this sort of community. As a result, you look forward to being with other like- minded people on the same journey as you, which can help to motivate you as well! There's no reason why this cannot be longer, like a whole morning of working together divided into sections where participants can get up to get a cup of tea or snack. The use of soft background music works for some people too. This can encourage your brain flow which makes it much easier to get on with any tasks.

Environment

As each person is different, not all environments will be suitable for you. Some people cannot have any sound, not even soft music, whereas others can. Sitting on the porch overlooking the garden is good for certain people. Taking a walk, driving to a cafe, and working on a laptop is another method, I have heard, that works. The list is countless. Use what works for you and be consistent.

In an office proper lighting and heating are ideal. Working in a windowless room with harsh light is hard on the eyes and emotions. Keeping a room on the cooler side and wearing a cardigan is preferable to a warmer room as it can affect concentration.

CHAPTER 9

PROCRASTINATION

"Procrastination is the act of delaying or putting off tasks until the last minute, or past their deadline. Some researchers define procrastination as a "form of self-regulation failure characterised by the irrational delay of tasks despite potentially negative consequences."

"A survey in 2015 found that, on average, a person loses over 55 days per year procrastinating, wasting around 218 minutes every day doing unimportant things. Here's the maths:

218 minutes/day x 365 = 79570 minutes = 55.3 days" Life Hack" (Ho, 2022)

That's mind blowing! When put that way, procrastination becomes an enemy to conquer!

You have probably never "snoozed" your alarm. You're too smart for that! I have done it several times. Thankfully not so much lately. Sigh! It is human nature to leave things at the last minute. I'm in a group of entrepreneurs and we were supposed to launch our businesses with in a 10-week period. Over 500 people managed to do this however ¾ did it on the last day, that with a lot of help from other registrants, plus sweat and tears.

This is a typical human behaviour, and most people fall into this category. My sister Alice is different. She had 4 children and was very organised in how she looked after them. It would always amuse me, in our young mum days, how she would finish getting ready before me despite that I only had one child.

Her shopping habits were just the same. By October she was always nearly ready with her Christmas grocery shopping. On the other hand, my groceries were done in December with some last-minute dash on Christmas eve. I was hardly ever late for work, unless something drastic happened but I had a different way of operation compared to her. I hasten to say as I have grown older there is more order in my life than then. Thank God!

There is an interesting law that enlightens the behaviour of most people. It is called Parkinson's Law.

What Is Parkinson's Law?

In 1955, Cyril Northcote Parkinson, a famous British historian, management theorist, and author, claimed that:

> *"Work expands to fill the time available for its completion. This suggests that if you proactively give yourself time constraints, you will be able to get more work done in less time. For example, if you allow yourself a week to finish a task that should take three hours, then (psychologically) the task will expand in complexity and seem more difficult, and it will fill the entire week.*

While it might not fill the entire time with more work, you will have an increased amount of stress and tension about finishing the task for the entire week.

This may explain why students choose to cram before exams, or why people complete projects at the very last minute of your tasks. But if you can assign the right amount of time to each you can gain back time, and the tasks will not seem so complex." S.J. Scott

I think that this is a good hack, do you? If you know that human nature will perform better with a deadline, then it is helpful to try this out, starting with easy tasks then going on to complex ones. In other words, you are informing your brain that we are not here all week, we only have 4 hours to complete this task. That should make your brain pay attention to rally all the cells needed to complete the task at hand.

Setting a reward is another way of getting this habit strengthened in your way of working. Some people will set a reward on completion and a punishment for not fulfilling the said task in time or not at all. The reward does not have to be a big thing. Anything reasonable, like a cup of coffee and your favourite biscuit before getting back to work. It is important to keep everything in perspective and not go down the route of self-criticism and condemnation because that would be counterproductive.

Embedding this into goal planning is a great way to keep motivation and there are fun ways for doing this.

Something like a 'happy clappy' song for completion and another for non-completion. Not everyone is for singing but you will know what works for you.

Other hacks that might be helpful for you include:

Setting Goals
This is an age-old practice to help with productivity. We do this unconsciously in daily life. However, in business this needs to be intentional and deliberate. A lot of people know about SMART Goals. Specific, Measurable, Achievable, Realistic, Timely. Unless a goal has a deadline it's just a wish. Years ago, people used to take anything up to 20 years to write a book! The shortest I heard of this year is 3 hours! The use of technology enables this, and James Malinchak teaches on it.

Chunking Down Goals
As I write this, I'm reminded of having a roast chicken Sunday dinner with the family. Imagine how taxing it would be to pick up the whole bird and take a bite, putting it down and another person does the same. Someone in the past must have come up with the idea of carving the chicken, sigh let the party begin. Bite sized goals are easier to achieve and avoid overwhelm.

Accountability Groups
Everyone likes to belong somewhere, even entrepreneurs. Groups come in various forms. For instance, live in- person meetings or social media platforms like Facebook or WhatsApp.

Activities and group sizes differ, sharing your intentions and things like posting your goals in a group is better than just working on your own without letting anyone else know what you are going after.

Closer relationships can end up being formed like friendships, affiliates, and the co-hosting of events. Two is better than one in most instances.

Masterminding
Most successful entrepreneurs belong to a mastermind. Some of these are high end and investments can run into tens or hundreds of thousands of dollars a year! The advantage of masterminding is you get advice from several other successful business owners. By the time you leave a meeting, you have leveraged solutions from several people to help overcome the challenges in your business.

CHAPTER 10

OVERWHELM

Being overwhelmed is being overtaken by thoughts and experiences. It's a feeling that there is so much to accomplish in very little time. A lot of time can be wasted in fretting about the tasks than in doing the task itself.

That's a biggie in business because some of the skills and tasks required are nearly all new. However, mindset goes a long way to minimise harmful effects like derailment or giving up. The question to ask is not, "How do I do this?" but rather, "Who has done this before, that I can learn from?"

There is always a way and there's always someone who has the answer to your problem. Forums, and freelancers on platforms like Fiverr and Upwork are great to assist in technology, drafts, logos and the like. YouTube is a great how-to platform which covers nearly every task of daily life and business. The greatest thing here is to ask for help.

Planning is crucial to getting things done and fulfilling goals. Once a plan is in place it is easier to see the path to follow. Breaking down tasks into 'bite sized chunks' is helpful in avoiding overwhelm. Each day one question to ask yourself is, 'What is one thing that I can do that will make everything else either easier or irrelevant?' Writing down the tasks the night before for the following day, can be helpful. As you put down the tasks in their order of importance this will ensure you are tackling the priority tasks first.

The Story of The Big Rocks

Stephen Covey tells a <u>story</u> about big rocks:

"An expert was talking to a group of business students. At some point in the talk, s/he brings out a big, glass jar, something like a five-gallon pickle jar. S/he fills it with big rocks and then asks the students if the jar is full. They answer "yes." Next s/he brings out a bag of pea gravel and pours the gravel into the jar. The gravel fills in the spaces among the big rocks. Asked again if the jar is full, the students are catching on and say probably not. Then the expert pulls out a bag of sand, pouring the sand into the jar. The sand settles into the small spaces among the rocks and pea gravel. By this time the students answer the expert's question with a resounding no. Finally, the expert pulls out a pitcher of water and pours water into the jar, up to the brim.

The expert asks the students what the point of the demonstration is. They respond that no matter how busy they are, there is always room for more in their schedule. The expert disagrees and says that if you don't put the big rocks in first, they won't fit."

You've probably heard this story before. It's illustrating the importance of doing the most important things first. In other words, make the main thing the main thing or 'major on majors' as the saying goes.

Lack of skills

This is expected especially when transitioning from a job to being a business owner because there are many moving parts. In a job you may have been an expert in a certain field, in business the buck stops with you. At the beginning you tend to be a jack of all trades but outsourcing and upskilling are a good way to overcome this. Being in a community is great in that skill sharing can be a great asset. Thankfully some of the skills gained in employment are transferable.

The Tech Nemesis

This problem just like above is also a mindset issue. Nowadays, software is so tailored that besides needing to know the ins and outs of SEO (search engine optimisation) and copywriting almost anyone can draft a website. Websites are not such a dreaded and expensive asset like they were a few years ago. Nowadays, businesses can use one-page websites, software like 'Click Funnels' which is a very helpful and predictive tool. Some teenagers are great teachers for parents in getting their head round some of the tech stuff. My son used to be my go- to person about 15 years ago. I can't tell how many times I kept asking him for help and occasionally you could sense frustration in his voice when I couldn't grasp a seemingly simple task.

Websites like 'Canva' are great for graphics to use for book covers, flyers, and cards. There are lots of templates too for almost anything to do with business.

Staffing issues

Online virtual assistants are a great asset to companies as they help the business owner to concentrate on working on the business rather than working *in* the business. With time you may need to hire staff for your business. It is important to hire somebody who has strengths in the areas where you are weak so that they can complement you in the business. There is training that can help you to know what the most important post is that you need for your business. Your coach or mentor will be able to assist you with this. As your business grows you will need more staff but by that time you are also growing as a businessperson.

Loneliness

There's nothing more enjoyable than a meal and a pint with the boys, or on a girls' night out! If you're a business owner who is working from home, oftentimes loneliness can creep in, which is why it's important to prioritise self-care. It's not so bad for people who live with family or friends but if you live alone, taking breaks for a walk, a call to a friend, video calling and meeting up in- person is always helpful. The other thing is to form relationships with like- minded people who are on the same journey with you.

Sometimes if your spouse or parents do not approve of you leaving the safety net of a job, you can be lonely despite living with other people. You can almost sense their 'I told you so' hanging in the air, especially on days when things are not going according to plan. It's a good idea to bring your spouse into the business at the start so they can support you.

Cashflow

This is one of the biggest challenges in entrepreneurship, especially for start-ups. The most taxing is likely to be the first 3-5 years. You probably know that most start-ups fold during this time which is a great shame. After putting in some hard work and effort no one expects failure. However, it does happen.

For your business to thrive you need a healthy and on-going cash flow. This is important from the get- go. Some sources of cash flow are family, savings, financial institutions, and city council grants. Other entrepreneurs prefer to work on a shoestring budget rather than borrow. Still others will choose business models that require minimal amounts of finance to get started.

Your market research prior to setting out will inform you how best to get finance if you have not saved up. No two businesses are the same, bank managers will be a great source of advice to point you in the right direction. Business Funding companies like 'Funding Circle' are some of the companies to research.

How can overwhelm be overcome?

Attitude of gratitude

We all have something to be grateful about. When you think of it, there is always someone who is having a harder time than yourself. Taking time to reflect on blessings is a great antidote to feeling low and unfulfilled. Most of the time we overlook people in our lives, daily things we possess that make life easier and countless others.

Having a gratitude journal is important to some people because it's a daily reminder. Writing this individually or as a family teaches children to think about the various ways to express gratitude.

Gaining Perspective

Is the glass half full or half empty? While two people are looking at the same glass, the interpretation is different. One is empowering and the other is not.

As already mentioned, it was during the Covid 19 pandemic that I heard John C Maxwell encourage his coaches to look at the world situation through a different perspective. He mentioned how there had been pandemics before and that this too will pass. Meanwhile we needed to pivot and keep taking action.

During the pandemic even senior citizens learnt how to use zoom. I have a friend over 80 years old who had to have 1:1 calls until she was confident to join a zoom prayer meeting.

CHAPTER 11

SELF- CARE

One important thing that some go getters neglect is self-care. It can be busy mums, wives, business, or professional people. It's a shame that they neglect the most important person. Have you noticed that airlines recommend putting oxygen on yourself before a child you are travelling with? They understand the parental instinct of saving your children but if you pass out then your child will not be cared for speedily.

At all costs it is wise to avoid burnout than treat it!

Prevention is better than cure. 25% entrepreneurs admit having suffered from burn out. Some of the causes are:

1. Not asking for help
2. Pushing at all costs -punishing deadlines
3. Perfectionism
4. Competitiveness

How can this be prevented?

The usual stuff like a good diet, balanced with fruit and fibre, adequate hydration.

It can be easy to get side tracked and be driven. But you don't want to leave your job and be driven. The result is gaining control and freedom.

Exercises like swimming, biking, hiking and being out and about are great ways to keep fit and have a break. There are a lot of fun ways to exercise with loved ones, family, and friends. Taking your mind off the challenges of business is a great way to relieve stress. Then, when you get back your mind is refreshed and ready to move on.

Know your limitations

Knowing your boundaries is very important! In business you cannot be everything to everybody otherwise you will soon burnout. It is important to have some structure to your day especially if you're working from home. Going to the office is much easier because you leave home behind and you're in a working space. But even with an office, you still need to know how to take a break and have healthy rhythms.

Social media

This can be one of the biggest challenges for having boundaries in your business. It is advisable to have a phone for the office which can be a landline and have a business phone that doesn't have any of your friends' contacts on it but, just business associates. That way you avoid the frequent 'pings' of your phone where a friend is telling you about this and that. This is likely to draw you in, get you side-tracked and lose precious time that is important for your business.

Family

Your family obviously needs to be able to access you at any time in an emergency. But it is important to explain to your spouse and your children and get them on board with what you're trying to achieve so that they can allow you the time you need to be able to get your business up, running and scaling.

Friends

Just like with family, your friends need to know top line what your goals are. It's very important to know who to keep close and who to let go as a start-up entrepreneur. Some friends will resent that you are no longer as available as before, or that you are changing and no longer the person you were before. While you may want to explain yourself, it requires wisdom to know who to share with and how much. This new baby may need sheltering from naysayers.

Fun time

Getting a business up and running can be monotonous at times, especially if you're working from home where there are no teams. It is therefore important to have your support team close. This could be having your spouse come and join you for lunch where you can have a relaxing conversation before you go back and continue working in the office. Or it could be getting your favourite takeaway and going to sit in the garden with the family and let the children play so you catch up with your spouse.

Taking vacation

Taking vacation is one great way to relax with family and friends. It doesn't have to be an expensive Cancun holiday, but perhaps a local holiday in your own country, like the so called 'stay cation' would do a lot of good compared to slogging on regardless. Involving the children in choosing a place to go adds to the fun. They love activities and their chatter and laughter are medicine to a hardworking parent.

Even checking into an Airbnb place for a long weekend would do a lot of good and taking walks in the fresh air is very beneficial. There are countless places where one could go and it's important to make sure at least twice a year that you take vacation and leave everything behind; the phone calls, the messages, and the challenges.

You-Time

This could be; taking a nap, walking, enjoying a jacuzzi, swimming, anything where you are undisturbed and just alone. For some, walking in the rain, sitting by a river or at the beach, with or without music. It just needs to be undisturbed time alone to regroup your thoughts, emotions, and even your life.

What are some techniques you use to re-fire?

CHAPTER 12

BENEFITS

One question that you may be asking is, "Why should I go to all the trouble of creating a business when I can just continue in a job where all the heavy lifting is done for me.?" Or "Why would I put myself under so much uncertainty when I can get a predictable salary." While you might not be totally happy with the salary you get, there is a temptation of choosing the area of least resistance. But this usually results in an unfulfilled way of life, where there is always a nagging feeling that there should be more to life than what you will be experiencing. Most people will settle for this and stifle the fire within until it smoulders down to ashes.

However, if you set out in determination to live out your life assignment, there is great satisfaction in facing life head on and finding meaning to your life. Anyone who has dared to do this has found that their yearning for more meaning to life was fulfilled. Not only that, but there is the wonder of how your product/service brings so much transformation in other people. Seeing your clients live a quality and fulfilled life is what makes you want to get up in the morning and pursue your goals.

Time, location and financial freedom are three other great benefits of getting into business. You can uncap your earnings and can decide what you want to get paid. All successful business people start 'with the end in mind.' They decide on the front end how much they need to make over a certain period. This could be annually or every quarter. They then reverse engineer and work out the numbers of their services to come up with the income of their desire. Being in employment is way different from this. The salary is pre-determined by someone for you. There is capping as well, which can be very frustrating. The salary raise is not much to write home about either!

Have you ever found that there was too much "month" at the end of your money? I've done that. It can be soul destroying which can cause a cry to rise within, "How long!" I cannot count how many times as an employee that I'd get to the end of the month or week and wonder why my money was so little because I had overlooked some deduction or other and found myself scraping the bottom of the barrel.

As a businessperson you can steadily build up your wealth, diversify and form partnerships. There's an African proverb – 'if you want to go fast go it alone, if you want to go further go with others.' Building a team around you helps with sharing the load and brings on other expertise to assist in growth.

I have seen many business partnerships who promote each other for launches. One business can have up to 10 others that are working alongside them to help with scaling.

Generational Wealth

One of the sure ways to build generational wealth is to diversify into the property market. Most millionaires are made in this area of business. House prices are steady despite the ups and downs in the economy. Most properties appreciate over the decades. Even during recessions, the property business has a way to weather the storms. House prices may drop too as people pivot to cope with inflation and rising costs.

Giving Back

Have you ever supported a cause and kept seeing more needing to be done but money and personnel were constraints? When you have success in your business it's the time to help others. The opportunities are endless from building schools for needy communities, to building orphanages and many other charitable deeds. This is what brings the most fulfilment as lives will be changed for the better.

One of the most inspiring stories is one of Scott Harrison who set up the charity 'water'. After living a life of fun, alcohol, drugs, clubs, and music for 10 years, he reached rock bottom and he "wanted the music to stop." He states he was spiritually and morally bankrupt. He applied to work with a humanitarian organisation but was turned down a few times, until he found one that asked him to pay $500 to be able to join them.

He became a photographer on a mobile hospital which went from the USA to Liberia. The doctor who conducted surgery on poor communities had stayed on the ship for 29 years. His work involved facial surgery on many people whose lives were then transformed in an amazing way.

While Scott travelled in the villages, he saw how thousands of people were getting sick due to drinking dirty water. These people were suffering from Cholera, Dysentery, Bilharzia. This moved him immensely. He stated 750 million people did not have clean water. The distressing scenes and stories galvanised him into action.

He went back to NY city and began fund raising by asking people to pay $20 for a party. Seven hundred people volunteered, and he sent the money to Uganda. The charity 'Water' was born and operated differently from any other charity. 100% of all money donated was used for getting clean water to needy communities. GPS was used for donors to see where their money was being used. Retailers, commercials, and social media were used to raise awareness. People started to donate their birthday money because they "didn't need any more stuff!"

Rachel, a young 9-year-old raised money - $220. She died in a car accident soon after and people everywhere gave $9 in honour of her, some climbed mountains, adults, even children joined in! More than $1.2 million was raised and 50, 000 wells were dug. Her family went to Africa to see the work. It was all very moving!

This is one man's story which changed the lives of thousands. No longer were young girls carrying heavy jugs of water and walking miles. Their school life was no longer disturbed. Preventable water borne diseases were a thing of the past.

Mother Theresa

Many people have heard of Mother Theresa, a Roman Catholic nun. She was working in a convent as a teacher in India, was well paid and had nice accommodation. But whenever she looked out of her window, she saw lots of needy people on the streets of Calcutta. These sites moved her heart so much that she had to do something. She left her job in the convent to minister on the streets to the multitudes of needy people. As time went on, she added a team of people who helped look after sick people. She was honoured for her work too. How many of us have seen distressing situations, and we tutted or shook our heads without doing anything? How would the world be if everybody that saw something disturbing did something about it, even just once? This world could be a much better place! Somebody needs to take some action. Maybe you tried reaching out to your MP and to the government, but you realised the buck stops with you. If nobody is doing anything about it, perhaps you could?

Usually when you are a business person it's easy to get support for the least privileged because you're not asking for anyone's money. But you are using your own money to either build a school or a house for a homeless person.

It might even be as easy as getting groceries for that family that lost their dad in a car accident. Or paying school fees for the children making sure they don't lose their education due to lack of funds. If you can do something, you can make it as big as you want or as conservative as you want.

Who will you impact? It's your turn to step up to the mark. What are you called to do? Will you, do it? Think of how many people whose lives would be transformed!

CHAPTER 13

CONVERGENCE

3 Circles of Convergence:

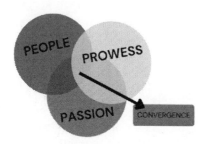

'Convergence' is a word I only got to know well in recent years. I vaguely remember it from geography lessons when I was in high school. But as an adult I first heard Dr Lance Wallnau teach that everyone has a convergence zone where the skills you have, the people you serve and how you serve them all converge like three circles. There's a small area which is at the centre of all three circles and if you work in that area, there is fulfilment because that is your sweet spot. He also says that people usually discover this in their 50s and only 20% of people manage to get into convergence.

So where is everybody else?

You don't know what you don't know, right? Who is responsible for educating others about this then? Getting into convergence is one of the best discoveries anyone can make. When you work in your area of strength you are like a fish under water or a bird in the sky. This is the place you were gifted to work in and you find problem solving, in this area, easy. Other people may struggle to come up with answers in that area but to you it's clear. You can just see it. This doesn't mean you will not need any upskilling; you do.

This reminds me of a conversation I had with my son. He said that from primary school up to year two in high school he never struggled with mathematics. He said, 'I just knew the answer, and didn't need to study this subject at all. But, in third year as the concepts changed, he said, "I began to fail exams, then I realised I needed to get a grip of this subject." That's the time he stopped failing in Maths. He added, "You might remember a time I didn't come home for Christmas when I was at Southampton University. I made it a goal to study Mathematics seriously and when the results came out the head of department asked me how I think I did, to which I responded, "I think I did ok." He replied, "You got the highest mark, well done."

Traditional Way of Learning

The education system was set up in America in 1830 by Rockefeller who is known to have said, "Give me a nation of workers, don't give me a nation of workers."

Here is an excerpt from the Medium which explains about the origins of the education system.

" Have you ever had the conversation that schools don't teach you how to think?

Have you ever been frustrated that you spend so many years in school and yet you come out with only the ability to regurgitate information?

What if I told you that independent thought wasn't the purpose of education in the first place?

The decades before and after the 1900's was the period of the Industrial Revolution. This is where many of the legendary billionaires made their fortune via the railroads, the automobile, oil, etc. The idea of the assembly line was crystallising into reality with the birth of mass production.

In 1902, The General Education Board was a non-governmental organisation designed to support higher education and was funded primarily by John D Rockefeller. Throughout his lifetime he donated approximately $180 million.

The board's objectives were to promote farming, to establish public high schools in the South and to develop programs for African Americans.

Why was so much funding put into schooling? What was his motivation? Rockefeller said, "I don't want a nation of thinkers. I want a nation of workers." Here is a quote by Frederick T. Gates, one of the members of the General Education Board:

"In our dream, we have limitless resources, and the people yield themselves with perfect docility to our moulding hand…. "

Phew! That's hard isn't it. When I went to school as a young girl, I never thought there were any sinister motives which we now read above. I was glad to learn, read, write, get to know my teachers, other students and quite enjoy the journey as well. But as an adult I can see the limitations in the education system. It doesn't give us the tools we need in the real world. Some people have gone as far as to say, "when you get out into the real world you need to unlearn what you learned in school and then start to learn what you really need for life."

That's a sad scenario because school should be the beginning of training for life skills. Areas like budgeting, savings, and investing, to name a few, should all be taught in school. It's not just about earning a degree which can just be worth the paper it's written on. But it should be about preparing you to be a winner in life and to leave a legacy. No one sets out to be mediocre in life, but we all want to know that our life matters, that we are here for a purpose and to serve others. When that is missing even if one manages to earn lots of money, life becomes meaningless. This is because fulfilment comes through seeing how you add value to other people's lives, listening to their stories and watching them metamorphose into the great men and women that they were meant to be.

So, it's important to get into convergence, to know what your passions and abilities are and get busy in changing the world. As we very well know you can't help everybody, and you can't change the world single handedly, but you have a part to play. So, unless you get to that portion there's a gap in society. That gap is shaped like you, so to speak. It's time to get into convergence and be the solution that people are looking for!

As you can see, traditionally the education system has a cookie cutter way of teaching. You are taught what to think and not how to think. You are given a subject and expected to spout it back to pass an examination. This is very limiting as you only work with what you are given, someone else's thoughts. Creativity is stunted as you need to stay within the box that is drawn for you.

Don't get me wrong, it is important for students to learn the basics in education. There is a place for that, however there is so much more within each person than just learning about ancient history, fossils, and geometry. These are short- changing pupils who have genius minds that need to be encouraged to dream.

Blinkers kept us going the way you were instructed. That's how everyone did it; parents, older siblings, neighbours, and teachers. So, we all followed suit. No one ever taught us about financial management, wealth creation and how to budget. The very everyday skills that were essential were never taught and as a result we got it wrong first before getting them right. Sometimes this was with lots of painful experiences which could have been avoided.

The greatest tragedy is that the education system is designed to roll out employees. You are trained to be the instrument in perpetuating someone else's dream. All the systems are set up to keep you in the lanes and wait for a salary at the end of every month. Some have gone as far as to say that a salary becomes an addiction.

That is such a shame as people could be better off living the life of their dreams, instead of staying in jobs they don't like, working with people who drive them bonkers, bosses who are taskmasters and get paid just enough to keep coming back. Robert Kiyosaki calls it a J.O.B. (Just Over Broke!)

Some people have discovered their sweet spot by accident when they lost a job, failed to find one in time and started thinking. Sometimes, the best thing you can do is to stop.

Henry Ford, 'Thinking is the hardest.... that's why most people don't do it.'

When you jump off the hamster wheel, the hypnosis wears off and you can dig into your creative gift and may be pleasantly surprised at the ingenious thoughts and ideas that you come up with. Suddenly you are aware of certain problems or gaps in solutions that you have a solution for. You devise your product or service, and then you find you are adding value to your clients, you have a business!

So, you may ask, 'What business can I embark on?' Three main areas to choose from that most businesses fall under are these main categories. It's not exclusive, but these are the main areas:

- Relationships
- Finance
- Health

Services like coaching, consulting, training, and mentoring fall into the above general categories. Products can be more varied, but these can get you thinking of which areas your passions fall under.

CHAPTER 14

SOME INSPIRING INVENTIONS AND BUSINESSES

The Wright Brothers

Every person was born to solve some problem, it's not just the superheroes. Think of people like the Wright Brothers who invented the first aeroplane for sustained flight in 1903. They lived in a house with no running water, no electricity, no telephone but it was full of books, lots of books.

Orville and Wilbur were born in Dayton, Ohio to Milton Wright and Susan Catherine Koerner Wright. Their father was a minister in the Brethren Church and went on to be a Bishop later.

The Wright children were educated in public schools and grew up, as Orville later explained, our curiosity might have been nipped long before it could have borne fruit. "There was always much encouragement to children to pursue intellectual interests; to investigate whatever aroused curiosity." In a less nourishing environment.

> "Bishop Wright exercised an extraordinary influence on the lives of his children. Wilbur and Orville, like their father, were independent thinkers with a deep confidence in their own talents, an unshakable faith in the soundness of their judgement and a determination to

*persevere in the face of disappointment and
adversity. Those qualities, when combined with
their unique technical gifts, help to explain the
success of the Wright brothers as inventors. At
the same time, the bishop's rigid adherence to
principle and disinclination to negotiate disputes
may have had some influence on the manner in
which the brothers, later in life, conducted the
marketing of their invention." Britannica*

From their bicycle shop, they began by building gliders
that often crashed! Then, together with their shop
assistant, they built a bi- plane which flew for 12
seconds at 120 feet. The Wright brothers knew they had
a breakthrough and went on to build again.

Prior to the bicycle shop they worked in printing where
they learnt problem solving whilst working with the
printing machines. They also published short lived
newspapers. One of their bicycles even had a self- oiling
hub!

From the outskirts of Dayton, OH, they invented the art
of aviation and were testing even more powerful
planes. They moved to Kitty Hawk, where the weather
and winds were more suited to their experiments. Their
confidant was Octave Chanute who was an aeronautical
engineer.

In 1903, they flew a glider for 26 seconds which went on
to fly for 39 minutes. There was no going back! They
knew they were on to something great. Work stopped

for some time so that they could get the patents and protect their invention.

Sadly, the federal government turned down their inventions and shut the door in their faces. However, France was interested and in 1908 crowds gathered to watch Wilbur take off in Lamont.

This made the Federal Government pay attention. They soon wanted to be part of what the Wright brothers were doing because they could see what happened when France opened the doors to them.

Soon enough both brothers were flying planes in France and America respectively. Orville took a passenger to have a feel of the exciting invention. However, sadly, this resulted in the first fatality when Thomas Selfridge, an army lieutenant was killed. Orville was seriously damaged physically and emotionally but was nursed back to health by his sister, Katherine.

> 'In November 1909 the Wright Company was incorporated with Wilbur as president, Orville as one of two _vice_ presidents, and a board of trustees that included some of the leaders of American business. The Wright Company established a factory in _Dayton_ and a flying field and flight school at Huffman Prairie. Among the pilots trained at the facility was _Henry H. ("Hap") Arnold_, who would rise to command of the U.S. Army Air Forces during _World War II_.'

This is an amazing story of courage, innovation, and adventure. We can see that nothing is impossible. Your dream will be realised if you too follow your inner compass, put in the leg work, and persevere.

Let's look at what made the Wright brothers press in to realise their dream:

- Healthy upbringing and support of their father.
- Ability and space to experiment freely.
- They began with what was easiest; bicycles, printing machines, then on to aeroplanes.
- Supportive partnership, neither of the brothers got married – I suppose they were too busy!
- They were focussed in spite of many setbacks.
- They tested different types of wings 200- 300 times!
- Hard work and grit.
- Studied aerodynamics and managed to stay ahead of the pack as pace setters.
- Overcame family challenges. Their father faced a lot of challenges in his work as a minister, but they didn't allow this to stop their invention prowess.
- Neither of them attended college, they were self-taught in a field that was not the easiest!

Their success shows that ordinary people can achieve the extraordinary if they put their hearts and minds to it!

CHAPTER 15

ARNOLD SCHWAZZNEGGER

Arnold Schwarzenegger was born in 1947 in Austria. He had a desire to emigrate to America and make a name for himself. His parents were not happy with his choice to be a bodybuilder, but he rightly pursued his dream.

He started his competitive career at 17 and in 1966 he won the junior Mr Europe and came second in the Mr Universe contest.

Here's how biographer.com describes his early life:

> ''Schwarzenegger was born on July 30, 1947, near Graz, Austria. Schwarzenegger's childhood was far from ideal. His father, Gustav, was an alcoholic police chief and one-time member of the Nazi Party, who clearly favoured Arnold's brother over his gangly, seemingly less athletic younger son. Gustav is reported to have beaten and intimidated Schwarzenegger and when he could, pitted his two boys against one another. He also ridiculed Schwarzenegger's early dreams of becoming a bodybuilder. "It was a very uptight feeling at home," Schwarzenegger later recalled. So uptight and uncomfortable, in fact, that Schwarzenegger would later refuse to attend the funeral of his father, who died in 1972, or his brothers, who was killed in a car crash in 1971.''

How to Unleash Your Greatness

Going to America became a dream for the young Arnold Schwarzenegger. However, with no money, there was a challenge on how to get there. With the help of a promoter called Joe Weider he was able to make his dream come true.

> *"Weider loved Schwarzenegger's bravado, sense of humour and the potential he saw in the young unprecedented five Mr. Universe titles and seven Mr. Olympia crowns during his bodybuilding career"*

Arnold went to America at age 21 with only $20 in his pocket. He started off working as a bricklayer during the day and at night focussed on his dream of making it in America. His sights were on Hollywood. He loved blockbuster movies, through a long process landed various acting roles including 'The Terminator,' which launched him to stardom. Do you remember the movie Terminator from back in the 80s? The other roles that he took were in 'The Rise of the Machines' and 'The Expendables.' One of Arnolds' greatest assets was that he was very popular with audiences.

Arnold was also interested in politics and served as Governor of California for two terms. His boldness in campaigning always came through and he stated he was inspired by President Ronald Reagan. He reported, "When I first came to America, the first president I voted for was Ronald Reagan."

Governor Schwarzenegger did not accept a salary, stating he was rich enough. As of 2020, he had a net worth of $400 million. A long jump from $20!

So, we see several things here from this biography. Let's look at some of the challenges that he had to overcome:

- A hostile family background where his father would pit him against his brother.
- The situation was so bad that he didn't attend either of their funerals. That speaks volumes of what their family dynamic was like.
- Getting to America from Austria for the poor 17-year-old was next to impossible, however Arnold would not be deterred.
- English was not his first language so that was a challenge. Getting to a foreign country and not knowing the language can be quite daunting for an adult, never mind a teenager.
- His home dynamics had not prepared him to be confident and comfortable in himself as it lacked love and affirmation.
- To get into Hollywood is a lot of people's dream but how many achieve that American dream? The road to Hollywood is strewn with bodies that never made it due to the rigorous requirements of being a successful actor. But we see this wild horse getting there and making the grade!
- How do you get from a foreign country and have somewhere to sleep that same day? Where do you start, especially when you only have $20 in your pocket? This shows that Arnold must have been very resourceful in how he overcame these odds!

- He was willing to start from the bottom doing the hard work of a bricklayer- which is backbreaking and looking for acting positions at night.
- Finally, he was elected to be governor in New York City for two terms. Anyone acquainted with the election process of governors knows that the competition is stiff and the bar is very high. Here, we see him again coming against the odds of being a foreigner and getting elected to quite a significant position in American politics.
- Help from Weider who saw the potential in this ambitious young man. This can happen for you too as there will be people that will see your passion.
- Due to his admiration of President Ronald Reagan, he was able to emulate his hero and become one himself.
- What his father lacked in raising him, President Reagan was able to provide unknowingly.

So, let's just pause here for a moment to look at what odds you find yourself up against. They could be more than what Arnold Schwarzenegger faced, but all the same you can glean a lot of good and gold from his biography. This can enable you to live your life in the direction of your own passions.

There are people you don't know yet who are going to encourage you to be bold and courageous in going after their dreams. You, in turn, will then be able to help and improve the life of others.

All I say is, I'm rooting for you to live your best authentic life and leave this world knowing that you squeezed every drop of that greatness that is on the inside. Nothing is impossible no matter your background.

CHAPTER 16

CHAPTER MARY ASH KAY

She left her job with a home products company after being passed up for promotion which had been favoured to a man that she had trained. But she went on to build a prosperous company, 'Mary Kay Cosmetics' by training and coaching women into confident salespeople who gained respect and was led to feel important.

Here's a caption from Biography.com...

> "After her bad experiences in the traditional workplace, Ash set out to create her own business at the age of 45. She started with an initial investment of $5,000 in 1963. She purchased the formulas for skin lotions from the family of a tanner who created the products while he worked on hides. With her son, Richard Rogers, she opened a small store in Dallas and had nine salespeople working for her. Today there are more than 1.6 million salespeople working for Mary Kay Inc. around the world."

The company turned a profit in its first year and sold close to $1 million in products by the end of its second year driven by Ash's business acumen and philosophy. The basic premise was much like the products she sold earlier in her career. Her cosmetics were sold through at-home parties and other events. But Ash strove to make her business different by employing incentive programs and not having sales territories for her representatives. She believed in the golden rule "treat others as you want to be treated," and operated by the motto: God first, family second and career third."

She invested herself in both her corporate and sales teams, thus getting remarkable success. In August 2019, the company was ranked to be in 'The Top 50' US-based companies in the Household and Personal Products Industry. It went on to be a $2.2 billion company! Mary's marketing and people savvy skills helped the company to grow. She called her salespeople 'consultants,' loved the colour pink which was used in the packaging as well as the Cadillacs that she gave away to consultants who excelled in business. Her consultants bought products at wholesale price and sold them for profit as well.

A lot of attention was gained to make this a way of doing business. Her business model was unique and prospered more than most during that time. Mary also benefited from the help of her son in creating the products. The business went public in 1968.

So, here is a story of a woman who was mistreated in the corporate world where a man who was junior to her was promoted instead of herself. Instead of wallowing in self-pity and feminism, Mary used this as the launch pad for her business. That's why she was interested in working with women; so, they too would gain respect in the corporate world, and gain respect they did!

Now it's your turn. It's the time for your story. What odds have you come up against that may be standing and looming in front of you and getting in your way?

Let's look and summarise how Mary overcame the odds that we are against her:

- She was born in 1918, that's my late grandmother's year of birth. This is two generations away and even three for some of us.
- There was no Internet maybe, no Snapchat, no Instagram, no Facebook, but Mary used what was available to her at the time to overcome the odds and to gain a reputation as a successful woman.
- She had no experience when she started off and her son was by her side to help her create these products. When you reach history on biographer.com it says she worked with a man who was dealing with hides of animals that's where she got her raw products. How amazing is that?
- Due to what she had gone through in the corporate, her sense of self-worth must have taken a hit, but she did not let the disappointment, or frustration stop her from following her dream.
- Unknowingly, there were women waiting for her success, as it were, so that they could jump on what she had initiated and discover their own purpose. They ended up as great women in

the marketplace. They were consultants instead of salespeople and drove Cadillacs!

We do not hear of Mary as having had an MBA nor attending Business School. But we hear of a woman who had good people and marketing skills. We see how she used what she had at her disposal to create an amazing business which still operates today and is still successful. She left a legacy of thousands of women walking in their life assignments and achieving impressive results.

Fifteen years ago, I had the privilege of attending a Mary Kay house party where one consultant was sharing about the products. I found her to be very professional and knowledgeable about her business. She did assessments on our skin to let us know the type of foundation that was good for our skin tone, including the cleanser, toner, and moisturisers. She talked about her faith as well. So, when I read the biography of Mary Kay Ash, I realised that that she has left a legacy with those people who are following in her footsteps.

You are at that place again of reflection and writing down the dream that you have. A place to pick up the desires you may have overlooked, passed over and thought they were too big and unachievable. Learning from Mary's experience can be a sounding board or a launching pad for you to start your own business.

It can be good practice to start off with a side hustle and then expand. Are you ready to jump into action?

CHAPTER 17

YOUNG ENTREPRENEURS

Quantum Marketer statistics (April 2022) states there are more than two billion active users monthly on Facebook globally, which makes it the biggest social media platform in the world.

Without going to other social networking platforms, that is a whole load of customers there for anyone who wants to communicate with the world! In other words, every day you can open your phone and speak to your target audience. No matter what age you are there are countless opportunities.

SELF- MADE TEENAGE MILLIONAIRES:

Nick D'aliosio

Nick is a self-taught programmer who used 'How- to' videos online. When he became proficient, Nick made his first app at the age of twelve and a few others later. Then at 15 he created the app 'Trimit.' He was financed by business magnate Li ka Ching to the tune of $300, 000 which solved the way news articles are read on smartphones. When the app was perfected, it was named Summly and Yahoo paid $30 million for it! They also gave Nick a position in the company.

Akshay Ruparelia

Nicknamed 'Alan Sugar' Akshay was selling houses while other kids were kicking the ball around. Yes, this was during the school lunch breaks. He avoided the school playground as he was quietly negotiating deals on his mobile phone!

He hired call centre staff to man his phone and he would catch up with clients outside of school hours. His company: 'Doorsteps' was valued at £12 million in approximately one year! Investors were trooping to buy shares from his company. WOW!

His company sold over £1billion in houses within 3 years! Akshay went on to become the youngest honouree of Forbes 30 – was featured in the Forbes 30 under 30 in Europe. His passion is to work with the disadvantaged, and he sits on the board of the Princes' Trust. Not only that, but he also started a social enterprise, AKR Growth, which supports unemployed people to get back into work.

Robert Nay

Robert is the founder of Nay Games. He built his way rapidly online by creating his gaming App 'Bubble Ball' at the age of 14. Which is a simple physics puzzle game. In the first 2 weeks it generated 2 million downloads from the App store. He toppled the No 1 App – Angry Birds and became an overnight sensation. The App has since been upgraded on Apple and now has created others under the name Nay Games.

Robert Mfune

Robert from Southampton was doing two part time jobs, at McDonalds and running errands, fetching tea for binary traders at a finance firm. As if this was not enough pressure, he was also at college. At the finance firm he got to know trading information through hearing the traders' discussions. He set up an account from home using his mother's name because he did not qualify to do so at age sixteen.

His mum was unhappy about this because he was losing money. When he turned eighteen, he opened his own account and learnt how to trade properly with the help of a good Samaritan. He initially lost money but began to make gains. He became a sensation when he made £2 million. He went on to buy a Bentley for himself and a car and a house for his mum. He is known for driving a gold Bentley, which his mum dislikes as she thinks it is too flashy! His net worth is around £1m.

Sean Belnick

Sean created Biz.Chair.com using $500 gifted by his stepdad to start an online furniture company, selling chairs when he was fourteen. When he went back to school his stepdad helped run the business and the two became business partners. They leveraged on the stepdad's experience working in the furniture industry. Business took off like a rocket and made him a multi-millionaire by the age of sixteen!

Their customers include Microsoft, Google, and the Pentagon. It has won various awards and was featured in the Inc.com 30 under thirty. When Sean was 20 his net worth was around 24 million!

Fraser Doherty, MBE

Fraser began his business venture at 14 when he learned to make jam from his grandmother in Edinburgh, Scotland. Fraser improved on the recipe by making jam from 100% fruit which he called Super Jam. Two years later he presented his Super Jam to Waitrose and got a tender to supply. He became the youngest person to provide a major supermarket.

This was not the end of Fraser's entrepreneurial prowess. He began supplying thousands of supermarkets around the world. His Super Jam teas for the elderly and Beekeeping projects are also well known.

Fraser is also a popular author and motivational speaker and has shared his story over five hundred times. He states:

> *"My story shows that what can start as a passion, with love and hard work, can grow into something amazing. Something that changes your life."*

He was recognised by the Prime Minister and was recommended for an MBE. In addition to all this, Fraser has a business called Beer52.

LESSONS LEARNED FROM THESE TEENAGERS

Created businesses using what they love. This is across the board from internet, furniture, jam, trading. So, passion is the common denominator here.

- Self-belief is deducted and perseverance.

- Age does not matter, just do your dance.
- Hard work and resilience.
- Doors open when you start and keep at it.
- The sky's the limit.

CHAPTER 18

FINDING YOUR NICHE

How do you do that? How do you find out who you serve?

This is in line with your passions and strongest convictions.

As mentioned earlier in this book, there are three principal areas of focus. Each area has several subdivisions.

The three primary areas are health, wealth and relationships.

Your passion will guide you on which one to choose. One way to find out what you are passionate about is to write out ten areas, trim it down to 3, then choose the 1 that resonates with you the most.

When I first ventured out from my day job to check out the business world, I was freaked out by the many unfamiliar words I heard being flung around in seminars and wondered if I would ever be able to cope with the steep gradient, as it seemed at the time. The worst was the marketing terms; squeeze page/landing page, funnel, drive traffic, paid ads...the list was endless. Usually, a smart Alec would corner me and quiz me on what I do and would have tough questions to try and show me how fuzzy my idea was.

I remember one time I lost it with the woman I sat next to during one training session. On the very first morning after introducing myself she asked me the usual question and said, "that business will not work..." She did not get very far because I cut her short and snapped, "don't you tell me what I can't do! All my life I have been told that by different people, and you don't even know any details!"

She apologised profusely and we sat in silence for 10 minutes. The moderator asked us to introduce each other to the rest of the group and when her turn came, she said, "This is Rose and we have fallen out already!" Today, we laugh about it and respect one other.

Why Is Niche Important?

Fast forward to last year, I was talking to one of my coaching clients and when I asked her who her target audience was, she responded, "Everyone and anyone who needs my help. I will not discriminate and will serve anyone." That seems like a grand and benevolent idea, right?

No, not at all!

I am glad to say after a couple of coaching sessions and going away to do her assignments, she now has clarity on who she is speaking to. She has created the most amazing product to serve single women aged 40-50 years who have been in abusive relationships, have lost their self-confidence and need hand holding to regain their confidence. She also formed a community for support and accountability.

The famous Zig Ziglar said, *'If you aim at nothing you will hit it every time.'*

This statement alone shows that sending out a broad message will have no one listening as each person who hears it will think it is not for them but the next person. A message that lacks clarity does not connect with the intended audience, misses the mark, and tends to vaporise. The presence of other products and services in the same pond will cause your message to mesh and not stand out.

Why Clarity?

Clarity enables deep connection and will cause you to stand out as the 'go to' person in the chosen niche market. Clarity causes you to rise above the noise and be seen and heard by those you serve. You may have heard the term, 'Confused minds don't buy.'

Nailing a niche means you 'get into your clients' heads' and can articulate their problem more than they could. It means you know and can describe what keeps them up at 3am. This demonstrates that you get them. You understand their pain, fears, hopes and aspirations. You can expressly show them the gap that is between where they are and where they need to go.

Finally, you leave no doubt that your product/service is the right prescription for the pain that they are experiencing. You demonstrate a step-by-step way of how this can be achieved. Then they come to you. You do not have to chase after them. They cannot wait to engage you as the provider of that service/product.

Potential questions that clients are silently asking.

"Do you care about me?"

"Do you understand my pain and struggles?"

"Are you able to help me?"

"Can I trust you?"

"Why should I listen to you?"

"Why should I listen now?"

John C. Maxwell authored the book, 'Everyone communicates, but few connect.' He mentions how he visited speaker after speaker and noted what they did well and where they did not do well. As a result of this he has become a well-known speaker and one of the best leadership trainers in the world. In certain entrepreneurial circles he is known as the best, I am just being conservative here! Maxwell's highest focus is on training leadership coaches, speakers and trainers to 'add value to people'

By the way, I have had the privilege of sitting under that training in person and have witnessed first-hand the team's practical outworking of that message too.

Getting in the head of your intended audience and describing their pain points better than they do is key to connection. Not only that, but also amplifying the problems and showing the price for inaction is crucial to get the attention of your target audience. One point to highlight with clients is this:

> *"If you think education is expensive, try ignorance."* *-David Rayden.*

But Rose, how do I stand out in a market full of other experts?

You are also an expert because of your uniqueness. Relationship marketing is the key. People will love you because of your quacks. They like you to take them behind the scenes and be in the loop.

The trick is to be your authentic self and you will appeal to people who do not care about a so- called expert down the road. To be effective you need to leverage your unique selling proposition. There is no other you. You are unique, use that uniqueness.

What is your story?

People buy from people they know, like and trust. Involve your family, pets, hobbies, struggles and wins with the audience. Be authentically you. Share not only your wins and gains but also your messes.

CHAPTER 19

FINDING YOUR IMPACTFUL VOICE

Everyone is different and the way we communicate best is different too.

There are entrepreneurs who love to write content through blogging, eBooks, newsletters, others love to train and will produce courses to teach people in their niche various skills.

Others always see gaps in information and transformation and love to train people in skills that edify their lives and that of others.

Mentors help you to shorten your learning curve and get to your goals quicker unlike when you work alone.

Yet others are comfortable with coaching and helping people overcome blockages and burst through bottlenecks.

Finally, there are speakers whose podcasts, platforms at live or virtual events are places of empowerment and growth.

Importance Of Coaching

Every person who is serious about personal development needs a coach. There are three main advantages of having a coach: S.E.A. (Support Encouragement and Accountability.)

Support

There is a saying, 'You don't know what you don't know.' Having a coach is important for support. Being a new entrepreneur is a giant leap which can be quite overwhelming, so the help of a coach is essential to overcome any obstacle you may encounter.

Encouragement

The business adventure requires encouragement because there are challenges that can just get in your way and trip you up. When this happens discouragement could potentially set in. A coach will help you to focus on your BIG WHY and to keep things in perspective.

The graph for a businessperson starts on a high then you go into the 'valley of death' In this place many give up and go back. That is the place you need the help of a coach the most, so you do not lose your focus. But if one persists then momentum does start to show.

Accountability

Any worthwhile venture requires accountability. This helps to push forward as you will have someone who can call you out on the targets you set. This is because we usually persuade ourselves to give up on our goals or postpone them. Accountability partners help keep you on your toes. This can be irritating at the time because there are days when you want to tell your accountability partner to leave you alone and let the business die. A good accountability partner worth his salt will ignore those pleas. They will exercise tough love.

Mentoring

"Mentoring is a relationship between two people with the goal of professional and personal development. The "mentor" is usually an experienced individual who shares knowledge, experience, and advice with a less experienced person, or "mentee."

Mentors become trusted advisers and role models – people who have "been there" and "done that." They support and encourage their mentees by offering suggestions and knowledge, both general and specific. The goal is to help mentees improve their skills and, hopefully, advance their careers." Mind Tools

I appreciate all the mentors I have had. They were in my corner and did not let me give up on my dreams. They still don't.

Public Speaking

Public Speaking can be virtual or at in- person events. Most people will voice fear of public speaking. Others have gone further as to say it's more feared than death! Public speaking is important when done well, to move an audience to your point of view in each subject.

77% of people admit to having anxiety about speaking in public, however when you take a leap of faith, the anxiety dwindles significantly. In public speaking you will also be encouraged to 'sell from the stage.'

Typically, speakers will have a table at the back to purchase a service or product.

Training

Trainers help you learn and develop specific skills and knowledge. They typically set the topic, the pace, the goals, and the learning method. While you will obviously choose courses that match your requirements as closely as possible, training courses, by their nature, start with their own agendas rather than with your situation.

Powerful Writers & Speakers

Steve Covey's book 'Seven Habits of Highly Successful People' touched many, including presidents of the United States of America. After his death this book continues to affect and transform many lives. The foreword contains 64 testimonials about how he impacted leaders from various walks of life, including:

Zig Ziglar:

Born in 1926 in a large family of 12, he went on to be one of the world's most popular motivational speakers, who influenced presidents, businesses and many millions of people. He wrote more than 30 books, 10 which became best sellers and won several awards.

Charlie 'Tremendous' Jones:

For 50 years, Jones persuaded people to improve their lives through reading books. He authored several books, including 'Life is Tremendous' which sold 2 million copies and was printed into 12 languages. He was a leader in the personal and professional development industry.

Your story is next!

CHAPTER 20

STEPS TO LIVING YOUR LEGEND

Here is a step-by-step formula which is a summary of the framework I created, 'The Profitable Passion Formula.' This helps take you from where you are right now to where you want to go as a business owner. I teach in group coaching sessions using this tool. (For more information, reach out to me via email, which is also located at the front of this book.)

Appraise

You may have had appraisals at work. Love them or hate them, they are part of most work environments. Your team leader will sit you down and appraise how you are doing and so will you, in relation to how the company is looking after you as a person. This is an opportunity to discuss career progression prospects, including courses you may want the company to send you to.

It is important to reflect on where you are in life, so you can account for what is working and what's not. You then get to celebrate your wins and change the things that are not winning. For you to be able to step into entrepreneurship you will need to look closely at how your work is helping or hindering you from feeling fulfilled and happy.

Successful entrepreneurs set aside regular times to reflect. This can be 2-3 hours a week. This time can be spent reflecting, journaling and course correcting.

Adjust

Once you know what is not working it's time to find an alternate route that will get you to where you need to go. If you are driving down a road and come across an accident, you would need to turn left, right, or even do a U turn to keep moving otherwise you could become stuck.

Mark Twain said, *"It's a mark of insanity to keep doing the same thing and expect a different result!"*

Once you have noted that Plan A is not serving you, it is time for Plan B. Here you begin to assemble something different. You get to say this is what I can focus on and create a business model that serves my target audience.

Audience

It is important to know who your audience is. No one can serve everybody. There is a particular group of people that your service or product is best for. Knowing who your target audience is saves you wasting time trying to sell to people who do not need what you offer. Done properly, gaining clarity from your audience will have people coming to you rather than you chase them. It is exhausting, right? This is covered at length in the previous chapter on Knowing your Niche.

Assemble

Once you know who your target audience is, you can then start to assemble content. You can do this confidently because you have done your research and know what keeps you target audience awake at night.

You know what their pains, goals and aspirations are and where they desire to be. This makes it easy for you to create a product or service that is like a key that unlocks the padlock of problems to set your clients free. All you need now is the best business model to deliver your solution. You also need to be able to articulate clearly how your product is the best to bring the transformation they long for.

Assess

This is where you get expert feedback. In every business venture you need an independent viewpoint. Coaches and mentors are much needed professionals who can ask you the questions you have not asked so that you get to sharpen your business idea. They help you create the best business model that delivers the best to your clients.

No one will take a piece of diamond from the field to the shop. There is a purifying process to get rid of the dross, so you have a shining product ready for launch.

Access

Once your service/product is ready, you need people to see, hear and know you. Not having a robust marketing plan means you could end up as the best kept secret on the planet. But you do not want that as you want to be able to transform lives through your product/service. There are marketing strategies galore, but your coach/ mentor will know what the best one is for you. You never have to invent the wheel but do follow what's working for you at any given time.

It is a recommendable idea to know your competition too. This is to see if there are any gaps or what they are not doing very well. That becomes your advantage. There is no need to copy everything, but you see what is working and then you make it fit to your product so you can say that this is your service/product. For example, if it's Instagram reels that are drawing an audience, you should continue, develop, and creatively produce your own and present them.

Accelerate

Every business has challenges, but it is possible to be able to scale with perseverance and time. For example, if you are coaching you could start by offering one to one and then go on to one too many! Then the next thing you could do is gather a team together. It could be one or two people to start off with. You can teach them what you know that already works in the business and the culture of your company. That way you've multiplied the efforts by having more people working on the business. In turn they mimic you, as they know what you would say and what you do because you've trained them well. Automation and teams can help a business grow and frees the owner's hands to work *on* the business rather than *in* the business.

CHAPTER 21

YOUR TURN

If you have come this far in the book it means you are looking for something. It shows that you are interested in taking back your finances, time and living life on your own terms. The biggest challenge is between your ears. If you manage to beat the gremlins and their snide remarks, the sky's the limit to what you can achieve.

I just want to say that it's never too late to start your own business. It's never too late to live the life that you really want even if it's just five years that you will be in business before you retire, those five years would be worth about 20 years of full-time employment!

Many people disqualify themselves for various reasons. Your life is the sum of the decisions that you have made throughout. Things don't happen to us, but things happen for us.

Many people disqualify themselves for various reasons. Your life is the sum of the decisions that you have made throughout. Things don't happen to us, but things happen for us.
Am I saying there is no injustice out there, or am I saying there is no discrimination? No, I'm not saying that, but the most important thing is how we respond to what happens to us. At some point we need to remove the ball and chain of the injustice, with help we can start living our life in a way that is free and fulfilling. We are relentless and unapologetic!

For example, we can choose to be people who magnify what happened to us and whatever it was or is that stopped us from following our dreams or we pursue the dream regardless.

We are relentless and unapologetic!

Reasons people use to exclude themselves:

- Not educated enough
- Did not qualify from high school
- Born to poor parents
- English is not my first language
- The government makes it hard for people
- The ruling party in politics does not care
- No one from my family has ever done this
- We are poor and survive on state funds
- I don't know how to use technology
- I'm shy, don't want to put myself out there

None of the above can stop you realising your dreams unless you let it. Sometimes the harder the task or the higher the bar, the more determined one becomes. Some people, although they are hard pressed, thrive on challenges and use the adrenaline rush to achieve the impossible.

Have you ever been behind an elderly person with a small butter, a couple of fruits and a ready meal and milk in the supermarket? It always saddens my heart. Some must choose between heating and food or heating and medicine. It should not be like that. These poor folks live a life of misery after working their knuckles off all their lives.

What about you? What will your rocking chair story be? Is it of courage and boldness or about how the system cheated you and promised a happy retirement after working hard most of your adult life?

This does not have to be your lot. Life *can* be different. Think of these people who overcame the odds that were against them. You have seen in this book examples of people from different backgrounds, age groups and genders. At the end of the day the only person that can stop you, is you!

Are you going to allow it?

In a training meeting, Paul Smith from Touchstone Education said if Nelson Mandela was able to change the face of apartheid and fight an uphill struggle against an establishment then you can achieve your dream.

Of late, unexpected calamities like the Covid 19 pandemic have left people jobless. Yes, some businesses have been affected as well but it is easier to pivot your business than employment because you are the one in charge. Someone else is not deciding on your fate. Your life is too precious to let someone else take the reins and drive it for you. It's time to take control!

Someone asked Elon musk why he is the richest person on earth, his answer was, "I read books."

Getting around people who have achieved the results you want is also an important factor.

Here are some examples from a book I read:

The Talent Code by Daniel Coyle

This book highlights how Coyle was intrigued by an exceptional ability in women's golf by South Korea, which was 33 of top 100 in the world. Moscow which was top ranking in women's tennis and one school system which turned 400% more students into college graduates. He saw there were talent hotbeds. Here there were people who tried and tried despite failure.

He discovered 3 foundational elements:

1/ Exposure moment- seeing someone like you excel. In 1954 Roger Banister broke the 4- minute mile barrier, after that other people believed it was possible and achieved the same result.

2/ Reinforcement- keeping the result you are aiming for at the front and centre of your mind. For example, visiting university as high school students and meeting under graduates from similar backgrounds. Then teachers encourage students and speak of their intended college attendance often.

3/ Need to belong- the fear of missing out or being left behind will spur others on, whether it's at school or in sport. Usually, younger siblings in high achieving families will push themselves harder so as not to be left behind.

It's the same for you. Once you shift your mindset and have a can-do attitude, you can achieve results which seemed impossible at the beginning.

CHAPTER 22

INTEGRITY

What is integrity?

MacMillan Dictionary says that integrity is the quality of always behaving according to the moral principles that you believe in, so that people respect and trust you.

> *"Integrity is honesty, generosity, being willing to do more than your share. We look for 3 things when we hire people. We look for intelligence, for initiative and integrity. If you don't have the later the first two will kill you."-Warren Buffett*

This, by far, is the greatest virtue that any businessperson can have. People will excuse failure, but they will never excuse a lack of integrity. Integrity will make your life, family, and business 'watertight.'

How do you model integrity?

Keep Your Word

In business it is important to keep your word whether you're dealing with customers or your business colleagues. An integrous businessperson will go a long way but lack of integrity will be your undoing. People have no patience with lack of morals because if you lack integrity how can they trust you or your service?

Maybe you've heard this saying, 'people buy from people they know, like and trust.' That's it, exactly! No one wants to part with their money to give to a character with dodgy behaviour. It is important if you mess up or miss a deadline to put your hand up and say, "I am wrong, I am sorry I didn't get it right." Your clients might be mad, but they will excuse you. However, if there is lack of integrity and you can't keep your word then you will never see those customers again. They may put bad reviews on your website or on google and bad news travels fast. You don't want that in your business. It's better to lose money while maintaining integrity than to compromise.

Turn up for appointments

If you make an appointment with anyone, make sure you turn up. There's nothing more irritating than making an appointment with someone and they don't show up. Always make apologies if you're running late and you can't be there the time set. Everyone is busy and can have appointments back-to-back. It might not be with business colleagues or customers, but they could be doing the school run picking up their children or attending a match that their child is playing in or picking up their wife from work. They don't want you making them late for their next appointment just because you couldn't get there on time. Now, it is a given that sometimes things happen, you could be caught up in traffic or an accident enrooted. Be integrous and always give the heads up.

Lead By Example

Leading by example is important so that you can be the role model for your team as well as for your customers.

We now live in a world where there is a shortage of role models. Whether it's in sports, business or in politics, role models are becoming an endangered species. As a businessperson you lead yourself first and foremost. You can't lead others if you are not able to lead yourself. It's not enough just to be a manager who gives out orders and ensures that every box is ticked. Your team is looking for leadership, not just a manager. In the marketplace most managers have got a bad reputation of bad leadership. So be different and showcase good leadership. This is especially important when you employ young people. How you turn up will make an imprint on their character as leaders of tomorrow.

Treat Others with Respect

Treating other people with respect shows good leadership. Anyone can be nasty and say horrible things to just about anyone, but it takes a man or woman of integrity to treat other people with respect. This is important, especially when you deal with customers from different backgrounds and from different ethnic groups. You need to show them that you treat everybody the same.

Personally, I have experienced prejudice in places, some shops or at the market. Those times are unpalatable. They leave you feeling frustrated and angry. I mean it's not 1888, is it? Showing respect is a sign of maturity.

So be a champion and an equality champion. Let everyone feel special when they come across your team, your services, or your product. You will not be hunting for clients; they will keep coming back because they know they are treated with dignity and with respect. This sells your product or your service.

CHAPTER 23

EMOTIONAL INTELLIGENCE

What is emotional intelligence?

Emotional intelligence is the ability to recognise, understand and manage your emotions and those of others.

Here is another way to look at it:

> *'Emotional intelligence is essential for understanding yourself as well as successfully navigating your social world. While some people tend to come by these skills naturally, there are strategies that anyone can use to learn and strengthen their emotional intelligence skills.'*
> *-Very Well Mind*

We have already seen how most of what we learned in school is not useful in life or careers. To avoid making an overgeneralization there are disciplines where what we learnt in university or college is useful but, in most jobs, you will not use that knowledge at all.

In the school system the emphasis is on intelligence quotient. However, in life, work and business, emotional intelligence will win the day.

Have you ever thought about whether it was necessary to learn about all you did in mathematics or other subjects, quadratic equations, Pythagoras theorem and all the other great sounding names? When was the last time you used them or even mentioned them?

The minute you walk out of that gate of your university or college into the real world then you need to learn new skills in new ways, otherwise, you will be like a square peg trying to fit into a round hole.

Areas Of Emotional intelligence include:

1/ Self-Awareness

Self-awareness is being aware of your own emotions. This is essential in how you show up when you're in the presence of other people. For example, you are aware that your mood is not so good because the children played up so much in the morning when you tried to get them ready for school. When you turn up to work you need to be keenly aware of that underlying irritation and deal with it. You need to leave it outside the door of your workplace. Your team at work has nothing to do with your parenting challenges. While they may empathise, they don't need you to dump anything on them. Inability to deal with this will result in demoralised staff morale which will affect productivity.

You may have had parents, teachers or bosses who took out on you something that happened to them before they were even in your presence. That sucks because you know you're not the cause of their foul mood, but you are just being used as a scapegoat. So be kind to your team and clients.

2/ Self-Regulation

Regulation is just what it says on the tin. It's a follow on from above, knowing yourself, your thoughts, your mood and cleaning yourself up, as it were, before you meet other people. It's the ability to show up as your best self for your own benefit and for the benefit of others. This fosters productivity of your team.

3/ Social Skills

This is a progression of the first two points above. People who are emotionally intelligent tend to be joyful and easy to get on with. They can form great interpersonal relationships because they are self-aware, and they are also aware of the needs of other people.

4/ Empathy

A self-intelligent person knows how to respond to distress, anxiety, or any emotional need in the life of another person. In other words, they are sensitive to hardship on behalf of others. They know how to say and do the right thing that will help to pep up the spirits of the next person.

5/ Self-Motivation

Lastly, emotionally intelligent people have got an inner drive. They know and understand their WHY, which helps drive them to fulfil their goals. They know that it is important for them to step out and step up as far as their intended destination in their business is concerned. They know and understand the reasons for procrastination and can sidestep these to fulfil their goals.

Here's how a workplace can create a clean atmosphere by having emotionally intelligent leadership and team:

- Safe environment where praise is given for work well done and some slack in areas where the work is not going as well as it should.
- Constructive criticism and feedback which is given to improve rather than to cut down the emotions in the spirit of the team.
- Team building exercises outside of work where people can unwind and be themselves. A greater connection is usually formed during these times.
- Allowing critical thinking and difference of opinion in matters concerning the business.
- Accepting other people's point of view.
- Valuing every team member and seeing them as equal human beings no matter what their colour, gender or level of education is.
- Avoidance of micromanagement, allowing creativity to flow.
- Making space for mistakes to be made and learning from them.
- Generous remuneration of your team.
- Rejoicing with their gains not just in the workplace but even in their personal lives. For example, if they get married or have a new baby or buy a new house.
- A happy team is a productive one.
- The work you put in will be generously rewarded.

- Don't let your tools be your machinery, your computers and such like, but let your greatest assets be the people that you work with. Most of the time people will forget what you said to them or what you did for them, but they will always remember how you made them feel. If your team feels valued, they will make you proud and are more likely to work hard even behind your back. These tips will help to move the needs of your business. They are soft skills, but they go a long way to ensure that you enjoy your time in your business and so does your team.

So how does one become more emotionally intelligent? Is it possible to improve on your social skills and become more self-aware? Yes!

There are tools that can help you to be more emotionally intelligent, so you don't lose friends, good employees or keep falling out with family.

First and foremost, you can take a test that can give you a score of roughly where you stand. It's easy to do because all you need to do is to search the internet and find software that can do this for you. The same software will be able to give you tips and clues on how you can become more emotionally self-aware.

Enjoy the journey!

CHAPTER 24

RESILIENCE

What is Resilience?

Resilience is the ability to cope with and recover from setbacks. People who remain calm in the face of disaster have resilience. People with psychological resilience can use their skills and strengths to bounce back after a setback. There are many setbacks we may experience; personal, family, and financial. In our case we are focussing on financial setbacks, how to avoid and/or bounce back when they are inevitable.

Statistics show that most start-up businesses fold within 5 years. Therefore, it is important to know how to build a resilient business, especially in times of recession which we have just entered in 2022. On the other hand, more millionaires are made during a recession than at any other time. So, the secret is to find out how to swim uphill despite the adverse situations that your business finds itself in. If others can do it, so can you! The only thing is to find out who is doing it, how they are doing it and then follow their example. As stated before, Tony Robbins always says, "success leaves clues." That means you're not without help and you're not without example. These can be your best days ever for your business.

For a business to be resilient the business owner needs to be resilient. Every organisation rises and falls on the leader. That's why in football when a team is not doing well, they don't fire the players, they fire the coach. So, before your business can be strong you need to be a strong character. For some this is an inborn thing but for others it can be learnt. There's lots of training and coaching around this subject.

So here are some tips to make you a resilient businessperson who can bounce back when adversity attacks. Preparation is very important. You already probably know that prevention is better than cure. It is better to avoid disaster than to pick up the pieces, right?

As stated in the previous chapter on emotional intelligence, having those skills will go a long way to help you be resilient. Possessing emotional intelligence skills helps you to avoid stress in stressful situations.

Here are some of the traits that you need to hone to build up a resilient character:

- Don't take yourself too seriously. One of my mentors always says you need to learn to laugh at yourself because everybody else is doing that. Life's too short to spend it like somebody sucking lemons no matter what is happening.
- Take everything in perspective. At the beginning of the 2020 pandemic, my coach was helping me to look at the situation we were in with perspective. He showed me how there had been pandemics before and wars too. He said what we were going through was not the first time something so bad had happened and that

it won't be the last. He continued to say that people in business had survived to tell the tale.

- Have a support system. This can be; family, friends, mentor, coach, or a group of like-minded people. Most of the time when you're a start-up business your friends will be your colleagues who are still in employment. They will not understand the challenges that you go through, so it is necessary to have a new inner circle of people who understand business, the challenges involved and how to overcome them.

- Having a coach or mentor helps you as I've stated above, about how our coach was able to help us make sense of the pandemic. It prevented us from being distracted by all the negativity and to concentrate on doing our business, using new techniques to pivot and be relevant in the new environment.

- Setting realistic goals or SMART goals as they are called, sharing them with your coach mentor and your group, going after them with all that you have.

- Asking for help when you need it, there's no shame in that. This will avoid a lot of hardship if done on time too.

- Having a positive attitude of seeing the glass is half full rather than half empty.

- Belonging to a mastermind, where you can get help to brainstorm solutions for challenges in your business. Most masterminds are relatively small and high end in investment. Most successful businesspeople belong to a mastermind.

- You always need to remember you're not Superman or Supergirl! You are not running on Duracell batteries either! You need to give yourself some slack, be kind to yourself and have rhythms of work and rest.

- Self-care, taking vacations, making time to have fun. Even if you have no children, spending time with your nephews' nieces or other children can help you to unwind and relax. Do whatever works for you. The beach is not everyone's ideal holiday place, do whatever relaxes you even if it's skiing in the Alps!

There is more to the things you can do to make sure that you are a resilient person. For instance, checking out books, podcasts, blogs on the subject will do a lot of good for you and your business.

Reading books is a great idea too! This is because you learn more, even from people who have departed this earth already, but who have made an impact during their lifetime. There's no limit to the material that is out there to help you on your entrepreneurial journey. Remember more millionaires are made during contrary seasons than at any other time. So, use the adrenaline of the hour to make your business great. You were born for greatness, always remember that. You've got this!

Real Examples of Resilience

- Jim Carey overcame homelessness, poverty, and initial struggle in his acting career, to become a famous comedian and the star of 'Dumb and Dumber' and 'The Mask.'
- Nick Vujicic was born without limbs, but is a very successful husband, father, mentor, and inspirational, international public speaker.
- Julie Marie Carrier of 'BeYOUtiful You' went from struggling to get money for a meal to being a world class mentor of girls. She has spoken to thousands and helped transform the way young girls see themselves, love themselves and find meaning in life.

'Resilience is one of the major keys to success. People who can overcome setbacks and stay on track will see more success in their lives than people who give up at the drop of a hat. By staying consistent and overcoming setbacks and disadvantages, you'll incrementally improve and set yourself up well to reach your goals in the long run.' – Chris Drew

CHAPTER 25
SEVEN TRAITS OF A SUCCESSFUL ENTREPRENEUR

1/ Love What They Do

The difference between working in a job and having your own business is that in a business you are working in an area that you love. I suppose it's safe to assume that prior to you getting into business you sat down and really thought about what you're passionate about and then went on to create your business in line with your passion.

By doing that, no matter how hard things might get, if you're working in an area you are passionate about, it will give you the desire and stamina to carry on. Your love for what you do will make whatever sacrifice or investment you make seem minute. That is why in a previous chapter we talked about the 'Profitable Passion Formula' where you turn what you love into business so that you are working in an area of your passion but also getting paid while you do that, so it's a win-win situation! It's like hitting two birds with one stone!

2/ Passion to Help People

A passion to help people is the next compounding reason why entrepreneurs are persistent in pursuing their goals. Seeing the transformation that happens in other people's lives because of their service or your product is very fulfilling to a businessperson and that becomes the fuel that helps them to keep going despite any hardships. Getting great reviews is good for the business itself but nothing is coming to shake your hand and thank you. For those that have students, seeing them excel and even surpass the coach in their achievements is a great thing to experience. If the trainer is comfortable in their own skin, it's great to celebrate together.

3/ Visionary

Being a visionary as a businessperson helps you to focus ahead on your goals. It doesn't matter how hard things may get; you will always find a way if you can't blast through it you will go around it to get to where you need to go. The great book says without a vision people perish. It is vision that keeps your dreams alive and gives hope and expectation.

Some great examples are:

William Ford, who had a desire to see every family in America own a vehicle. At that time cars were very expensive, but he set out to design a vehicle that would be affordable for families. He had a firm belief that it was possible, and he achieved his dream and desire.

Steve Jobs' promise of 1000 songs in your pocket seemed ridiculous at the time that he mentioned it. But the iPod became a reality and people ditched the Walkman and all went for the iPod. Later the iPod was booted by the iPhone, one man's dream changed nearly the whole world.

4/ Risk Taker

Business involves taking risks. This is a follow on from seeing the vision just like we mentioned above, after Steve Jobs saw the vision of the iPod. He had to take certain risks and the first was to speak it out to people. Some scoffed at the idea; however, they are not scoffing anymore, are they?!

Without taking risks, once you sentence yourself to your comfort zone, you will only do what you've always known. But all successful entrepreneurs will take risks at one point or another. Without taking risks the world would be doomed to stay in a dull, dreary, and mediocre world. But thank God, the world we live in is full of innovation, colour and variety which is quite refreshing to behold.

5/ Good Communicator

Good communication is one of the greatest assets that a successful businessperson requires. It is mentioned in a previous chapter on emotional intelligence. As a business owner you need to articulate how your product or service will help the client and bring the transformation that they are looking for. There needs to be clarity or a step-by-step explanation that leaves the client in no doubt that you are the person that can help them when they come to solve their problem. You've probably heard the term 'a confused mind doesn't buy,' so having persuasive skills without being salesy is very important to win customers.

Besides customers, you also need to communicate with your affiliates so they understand how your product service helps your target audience before they can help you to market this to their own audience. Your affiliate partners would want to maintain their integrity and reputation with their customers so they will not take up your service or product unless there is seamless communication.

6/ Long Term Goal Setter

In business I've heard coaches say that most people underestimate how much can be achieved in the long term and overestimate what can be achieved in a workshop, training event or in the short term. The law of compounding is what helps you as you take consistent action to achieve your goals. What you do daily is very important to keep the needle of your business moving forward.

As much as life events can be exhilarating and exciting they can only go so far, you still need to work day by day for great results. You will start to see some results after some time despite initially not really seeing any change. This is where perseverance comes in. Remember the story of Thomas Edison who did 1000 experiments to create the light bulb? He never gave up, so you shouldn't either.

7/ Manage Finances

It is imperative for the start-up entrepreneur to be savvy with their finances. Not everyone loves jiggling with numbers but in business it's unavoidable. One of the founders needs to deal with finances and as the company grows, this can be outsourced, or you can employ an accountant.

Some of the areas that need to be flawless are the following:

- Good invoicing and follow up of payments.
- Pricing goods and services competitively in comparison to the industry.
- Cash flow projections, reviews and course correction.
- Keeping expenditure reasonably in check.
- Avoid borrowing where possible.

One of the main reasons 75% of start-ups fail within the first 5 years is due to lack of funding. Some sources of funding are the bank and other financial institutions, friends and family and self-funding. Some City Councils offer grants, which can also be helpful.
My mentor calls your job 'the angel investor.' You may need to work and do your business on the side in the early days.
Your bank manager can help you with financial advice or else you can engage an accountant to help you deal with the figures. This is crucial as your business will fail if this area is not adequately addressed. There's a lot of help there, all you need to do is ask.
The above list is not exhaustive concerning the requirements of office setup, but these are some of the pertinent issues. In this internet age, help is at your fingertips!

ONE LAST MESSAGE

"The opportunities are endless,
now it's your time to act!"

Special <u>FREE</u> Bonus Gift for You

ATTENTION PROSPECTIVE ENTREPRENEUR!

IT'S TIME TO ESCAPE THE JOB GRIND!

Do you feel :-

- Stressed and frustrated in your day job?
- Unappreciated and overdue for promotion?
- Or you have reached the ceiling and there is no more growth to experience?
- You have a passion but lack the skills to translate that into a thriving business?
- You need support and accountability partners to reach your goals?

Then this is for you...

to help you to achieve success:

Https://lookhigherplatform.coachesconsole.com

References

Be Fulfilled, 2022, Be Fulfilled Journal, Available Online: https://www.tonygrebmeier.com/befulfilled-journal Accessed on: 13/10/2022

Chad Allen, Available online: https://www.chadrallen.com/ Accessed on: 13/10/2022

Chris Drew PhD/ Resilience https://helpfulprofessor.com/resilience-examples 2022 - Accessed online 01/11/22

Cyril Northcote Parkinson. Parkinson's Law/ How to Use Parkinson's Law to Get More Done in Less Time - Lifehack Accessed online 02/11/2022

Daniel Coyle. The Talent Code. https://danielcoyle.com/the-talent-code Coyle provides parents, teachers, coaches, businesspeople, with tools they can use to maximize potential ...Available on line – accessed on 03/11/2022

David Rayden - If you think education is expensive, try ignorance. https://davidrayden.com Accessed online 08/11/2022

Dr Myles Munroe – The Wealthiest Place on Earth - God Seeker TV, 2021 Available online. Accessed 02/11/202 Drew, Christ, 2022, Helpful Professor, Available online: www.Helpfulprofessor.com Accessed on: 14/10/2022

Thomas Eddison 2015 https://due.com/blog/thomas-edison-, 10000-ways-that-wont-work Accessed online 09/11/2022

Education Board origins in 1930/USA 1930
www.medium.com available online. Accessed
08/11/2022

Education cost - https://www.whebgroup.com/our-
thoughts/if-you-think-education-is Accessed online
3/11/2022
Elon Musk www.indy100.com/celebrities/elon-musk-
favourite-books-list Accessed online 10/2022
Emotional Intelligence – https//verywellmind.com -
Available online. Accessed on 26/09/2022

Fraser Docherty, Super Jam
speakersden.co.uk/speakers/fraser-doherty-78/
Accessed online 22/10/2022

Henry Ford
https://www.entrepreneurpost.com/2021/11/08/whet
her-you-think-you-can Available online. Accessed
08/11/2022

Ho, Leon, 2022, '5 Types of Procrastinators: Which Type
Are You?', in *Lifehack,* Available online: Accessed
14/10/22
https://www.lifehack.org/articles/productivity/types-
procrastination-and-how-you-can-fix-them.html

Jack Canfield - Everything you need is on the other side
of fear. Accessed online 01/11/2022.
https://undefeatedmotivation.com/quotes/everything-
you-want-is-on-the other side of fear

Jim Rohn
https://www.goodreads.com/quotes/403677
15/10/2022 · "Don't wish it was easier wish you were
better. Don't wish for less problems wish for more skills.
John C. Maxwell's books:

-The 15 Invaluable Laws of Growth –2012. Five frogs on a log, - Everyone communicates, few connect. Book, 2010.

Joyce Meyer. Do it Afraid https://www.churchloaded.com/books/ Available on the internet. Accessed 08/11/2022

Life Hack (Ho 2022) "A survey in 2015 found that, on average, a person loses over 55 days per year procrastinating. Available online. Accessed 08/11/2022

March, Nacine, 2020, 'How to create a habit (3 lasting steps!)', in *The Content Leader*. Available online: https://thecontentleader.com/create-habit-3-lasting-steps/ Accessed on: 14/10/22

Mark Twain - The Apocryphal Twain 2016- The two most important days. Available online Accessed 03/11/2022

Mary Kay Biography www.Biography.com – accessed 08/11/2022 online

Mentoring Available online. Accessed -01/11/2022 www.mindtools.com/pages/article/newCDV_72.htm

Mike Kim, 2022, Available Online: https://mikekim.com/ Accessed on: 13/10/2022

Patel, 2022, 'What is the Pomodoro Technique & how does it work?' in Project Management, Available online: https://project-management.com/pomodoro-technique/ Accessed on: 13/10/2022

Psychreg, 2021, '77% of People in the UK Experience Imposter Syndrome', in *'Psychreg'*, Available online:

https://www.psychreg.org/people-uk-experience-imposter-syndrome/ Accessed on: 13/10/2022

Scott Harrison Online, accessed 09/11/2022 https://www.charitywater.org/

Watch how a radical decision to reset his life led Scott Harrison to build charity: water.
Stephen Covey https://www.mgmtstories.com/ . The Big Rock Story. available online. Accessed on 08/11/2022

The number of online users April 2022, Quantum marketer.com accessed online 20/10/2022
Suzy Kassem, 2021
https://www.goodreads.com/quotes/9477633-fear-kills-more-dreams-than..2021 Available online. Accessed on 02/11/2022

Schwarzenegger was born on July 30, 1947, near Graz, Austria. www.biographer.com Accessed online 02/102022

Theodore Roosevelt
https://www.goodreads.com/quotes/597800-far-better-it-is-to-dare   Accessed online 02/11/2022

Warren Buffet https://www.rosterelf.com/blog/warren-buffet-wisdom-hiring-staff - Accessed online 02/10/2022

Lance Wallnau/Convergence, 2020 Accessed on line on 09/11/2022 https://lancewallnau.com/how-to-live-in-the-convergence-zone

Wright Brothers Biography www.britannica.com/biography/Wright-brothers/Going-into-business/2018 Available online. Accessed 01/09/2022

Yvon Chouinard Fear of the Unknown https://www.quotes.net/mquote/961999 Available online/Accessed 02/11/2022

Zig Ziglar – If you aim at nothing, you will hit it every time. Accessed online 03/11/2022 https//blingacademy.org/2020/07/02/f-you-aim-at-nothing-you-will-hit-it-every-time/

Printed in Great Britain
by Amazon

14283882R00086